Clive of India

Other books by the same author

The Enemy Within

The Unexpected Angel

Common Love

Leopard With a Thin Skin

The Quarrelling Room

The Glass Façade

He Also Served

Clive of India

John Watney

SAXON HOUSE

SAXON HOUSE,

D. C. Heath Ltd.,

Westmead, Farnborough, Hants, England

© John Watney 1974

ISBN 0 347 00008 8

Library of Congress Catalog Card Number

Printed in Great Britain by
Robert MacLehose & Co. Ltd
The University Press, Glasgow

Contents

Part One

The Making of Clive

Chapter 1

The Booby

'After all, the Booby has sense.'

Robert Clive's father, Richard Clive, was to say this later on when his unpredictable eldest son had made good. But for the greater part of his childhood the future victor of Plassey was, it must be admitted, a great trial to his family, friends and neighbours.

He was born on 29 September 1725 at Styche in Shropshire. The small half-timbered Elizabethan manor house stood in a hollow in damp marshy land a mile and a half west of Market Drayton. It had belonged to the Clive family since the time of Henry II, that is to say, some five hundred years before Clive was born. The estate, however, was small, and the Clives, though an old family, did not carry much power in a county that abounded with large estates and a strong 'back woodsman' mentality.

Robert was baptised at St Margaret's Church, Moreton Say, on 2 October 1725. The church, then still presenting the earlier Saxon appearance, stood about a mile south-west of Styche in the even lower-lying marshy land known as Smythmoor. It was a decrepit church and considered unsafe. Indeed, the whole area, with its draughty, uncomfortable houses, its creeping mists, damp fields and squelchy morasses, had fallen far behind the bright progressive eighteenth-century ideas. It was an area allowed to rot away under its own wet sun.

His father struggled to keep the estate together on a family inheritance of £500 a year. It was barely enough to pay for the upkeep of the old buildings, constantly in need of repairs.

In order to increase his income, he took on legal work. Like a number of other members of his family, he had been trained as a lawyer. But he had the unfortunate habit of generally losing the cases he defended, or else lending money to absconding borrowers. In consequence, the Styche estate was heavily mortgaged, and the debts mounted right from Robert's birth.

Clive senior's temper was never very good. His lack of money and legal success made him increasingly irritable. His growing family did not improve matters. And Robert, the eldest, was a difficult and noisy child, full of a strange and restless energy, that gave his small face a determined and pugnacious look. Only his brown eyes showed that behind the belligerent exterior lived a shy and sensitive being.

By 1728 Robert Clive's mother, Rebecca, had given birth to two more babies. She was, in fact, to have thirteen children in all, six sons and seven daughters. She was very much aware that her noisy and turbulent eldest son irritated his father to an unusual degree. Though she herself loved her son, she could see that something would have to be done, if the family were not to disintegrate completely. But what?

The solution came from an unexpected source. Rebecca had two sisters. One had married the eleventh Lord Sempill. The other, Elizabeth, had married Daniel Bayley in 1717, at the age of seventeen.

Daniel Bayley was a successful Manchester businessman. As he himself once wrote: 'Pretty good Trade makes us busy.' The Bayleys lived at Bayley's Court, Market Place, Manchester.

But, although they had been married ten years, they had no children of their own, and it seemed unlikely now that they would have any.

One day, when Elizabeth was visiting her harassed sister at Styche, she suggested, half jokingly, that she, who could have no children, should take one from Rebecca. The one she had her eye on was the lively eldest boy, Robert. Something about him had, from the very beginning, attracted her.

The sisters were Gaskells, and came from a strong non-Conformist family that had been in business in Manchester and Bury for generations. They were accustomed to making decisions, and sticking to them. To Rebecca, Elizabeth's offer came at the right moment.

After a certain amount of family discussion, it was decided that Robert should live with Aunt Bay, as Elizabeth now began to be called. Both she and Daniel Bayley were delighted with their newly acquired three-year-old boy, and began to give him all their love and devotion.

This devotion was soon to be put to the test, for within a few months of arriving in Manchester, young Robert contracted, just before Christmas 1728, one of those mysterious 'fevers', in this case to the abdomen, that killed so many young children at the time.

He was put to bed, the doctor was called, medicine was prescribed, and each foster parent took it in turns to stay with the invalid. Daniel Bayley would even lie full-length on the bed beside the child to hold him during the dreadful shuddering fits that almost tore him apart.

Daniel wrote nearly every day to his friend the Reverend King, vicar of Styche, giving him the latest news of the boy's progress, and asking for this information to be passed on to his sister-in-law.

On Saturday, 18 December, the crisis seems to have been reached. In his letter dated that morning, Bayley wrote: 'If I were given to be superstitious and to believe in things ominous, I think I should omit writing to you; for it has been poor Bob's fate to grow worse, just after I have finished my letters.'

However, the crisis passed, for two days later he was able to inform the vicar that Bob was much better, and as a sure sign of this added, 'his exceeding patience is also exchanged for an eminent degree of crossness'. The letter had to be brought to an abrupt end for 'I am writing this close to his bedside, and he is crying with the greatest impatience for me to lie on the bed with him; nor will he be quiet one moment, with all the fine words I can give him. . . .'

By the end of January, the child had recovered sufficiently for Daniel Bayley to write: 'Yesterday Bob came down into the parlour for the first time. He goes on successfully with the bark [quinine], and is very merry and good as it is possible. He is poor and thin; but in a brave way, and has stomach for more meat than we dare give him. He can run about, and chatters continually, and is always asking questions. . . .'

No doubt the boy was spoilt by these two gentle and loving foster parents, He was the centre of grown-up attention, whether he was well-behaved or not. His future, his education, his clothes, his pastimes were constantly under discussion and review. His health was watched carefully in case there was a return of the fever. He was still a rather delicate child, not growing very fast. He was to have for the rest of his life a delicate constitution. It's not surprising that he was able to get his own way with the easy-going foster parents.

As he grew older, he became more and more fond of fighting. He would pick quarrels whenever he could. It did not matter whether the boys were older, bigger or stronger, as long as they would fight.

Distractedly, Daniel Bayley wrote to his friend at Styche:

'He has just had a suit of new clothes, and promises by his reformation to deserve them. I am satisfied that his fighting (to which he is out of measure addicted) gives his temper a fierceness and imperiousness, that he flies out upon every trifling occasion: for this reason I do what I can to suppress the hero, that I may help forward the more valuable qualities of meekness, benevolence and patience.'

But Bayley could no more control this fierce little boy of seven than many stronger men were later able to control the man he was to become. There was in him already a fundamental force struggling to emerge, finding only in the fists of other boys a necessary outlet. The worst thing that could possibly have happened to Robert Clive at this time would have been for Daniel Bayley to have succeeded in curbing 'the hero' in him. Meekness, benevolence and patience may have seemed excellent attributes to good Mr Bayley. They would hardly have been of assistance to young Mr Clive. And no amount of beating would ever have tamed him.

Aunt Bay used to go to chapel in Cross Street, and would often take young Robert with her. The Gaskells had always been regular chapel-goers. They also took an interest in the running of non-Conformist schools. One of these was the Stand Grammar School.

It had been started in 1688, thanks to a tailor called Henry Siddall, of Whitefield, who left in his will four and a half acres of land. The small amount of income derived from these acres was just enough to keep alive a teacher of English and Grammar.

By the time Clive arrived there, probably in 1732 when he was seven, a new one-storey school-house had been built next to Stand chapel. Until then lessons had taken place in the chapel when it was not being used for religious purposes.

The headmaster, William Walker, was a relation of the Gaskells. His father, Peter Walker, had a house near the school, and here scholars used to board. Although not all that far away from home, Clive probably boarded in term-time with the headmaster's father. He was thus, technically at least, still within the family orbit.

There is no record of what progress, if any, he made under William Walker's tuition. There is a rumour in the school today, where a magnificent plaque to Clive was unveiled in 1913 by one of Daniel Bayley's descendants, Sir Steuart Colvin Bayley, that he was expelled. But this is unlikely.

What happened was that he left the school suddenly in 1735, when his much loved Aunt Bay died at the early age of thirty-five. Clive was not then ten.

Daniel Bayley, now a widower, could no longer keep the aggressive boy. Clive had never had the same feeling for good Daniel as for Aunt Bay, a fact that Daniel knew only too well. In one of his many letters to the Reverend King, Daniel wrote that he hoped the boy 'regards me, in some degree, as well as his Aunt Bay.' But Bayley's Court would not be the same without Aunt Bay. Sadly, Daniel Bayley returned the little boy to his parents.

In years to come, Clive was to sigh for his 'dear delightful Manchester' and write in one of his letters from abroad: 'If I should be so far blest as to revisit again my own country, but more especially Manchester, the centre of all my wishes and all that I could hope for or desire would be presented before me in one view.'

Once at home, however, the problem of his education had to be faced.

He was sent to a school in Cheshire run by a Dr Eaton.

Clive soon showed that he had a positive hatred of academic work, or indeed of book-learning of any kind. He skipped his lessons as much as possible, and just went on fighting in his usual way.

Yet Dr Eaton made the following memorable prediction: 'that if his scholar lived to be a man, and opportunity enabled him to exert his talents, few names would be greater than his.'

It is an unusual statement. Schoolmasters are not, as a rule, known to be very clairvoyant where their students are concerned. Many brilliant men have had terrible school reports. Then the wording is strange: if he lived to be a man. Was this a reference to the delicate health of this fierce boy? Or did the headmaster expect him to break his neck before long?

It would be interesting to see the reports Dr Eaton made out for his other pupils. Perhaps he predicted a fine future for all of them, partly to please the parents and partly to secure the future. He would not be the first, nor the last, headmaster to do so.

But this favourable, if somewhat ambiguous, statement was of little comfort to the boy's father. Richard Clive hoped that his son would follow his own example, and take up the Law. A disposition to throw his school books at the head of any passing boy was hardly a good start for a future lawyer. Slowly Richard Clive came to the sad conclusion that his first-born was no scholar. In his disappointed annoyance, he took him away from Dr Eaton and began to call him 'The Booby'.

One day, the people of Market Drayton, on passing by their church, were amazed to see a small but sturdy boy sitting on a stone dragon-shaped spout at the very top of the steeple. He kicked his legs, laughed, and waved to the gaping, breathless people below. He appeared to be utterly unaware of his danger. They shouted to him to be careful, to come down, to stay where he was. But he just went on laughing and waving as if climbing steeples and sitting on stone spouts was the most natural thing in the world.

He finally came down, when he was ready; moving with extraordinary ease and confidence over the stonework. When asked why he had attempted such a perilous venture, he merely replied that he had seen an interesting-looking stone lying on this spout, and that he wanted it.

His new schoolmaster, the Reverend Burslem of Market Drayton, could make no more progress with the rebellious boy than Dr Eaton before him, but at least he did not issue any startling prophesies. Nothing, it seemed, would drive any academic knowledge into the boy's head.

Clive was too busy with other much more exciting activities. He had become the leader of a gang. Under his orders were four or five other Market Drayton boys. They followed him wherever he went, did whatever he ordered. There was never any doubt as to who was leader.

Unlike the gangs most boys join, Clive's gang had a commercial slant. It was his first attempt at business, and it was extremely successful.

Clive's idea was, like all good ideas, quite simple: he and his gang would turn up in some force at, say, a sweet shop, and ask to speak to the owner. The shopkeeper would ask what they wanted and Clive, the leader and spokesman, would reply. He was offering, he would explain, protection.

Protection from what, the shopkeeper would ask. From my band, Clive would reply cheerfully.

Sometimes the shopkeeper would laugh, and as often as not give the boys a bag of sweets. But sometimes when they asked for money or more expensive items, the boys would be chased out into the street with curses and threats.

Clive would then immediately rally his forces, and counter-attack. His methods of persuasion were simple, direct and often effective. One group would attack from the front, lobbing stones into the shop windows, while another group would attack from the back, running through the shop, over-turning barrels and counters, scattering the goods for sale, before finally disappearing.

Later Clive would return alone, and put once more before the harassed shopkeeper his condition for calling off the attacks by his gang. There was no police or communally organised defence. As often as not the shopkeeper would pay up the small ransom for the sake of peace.

But not always.

One shopkeeper held out stubbornly against all of Clive's means of persuasion.

Something of a really drastic nature was needed.

Clive had a bright idea: it had rained recently and the gutter that ran down the middle of the street was full of muddy water. Why not build a dam, and direct the torrent, so that it ran straight through the shop?

No sooner thought than done.

The boys built the dam, and the water began flowing in a very satisfactory way towards the shop. There was little that the shopkeeper could do except curse and shake his fists at the gang.

But suddenly the dam itself burst, and the water began to resume its normal course. Clive immediately threw himself down in the gutter and blocked, as a certain Dutch boy was to do for more noble reasons, the breach, until his companions had repaired the damage and the water flowed once more towards its target. The shopkeeper paid up.

No doubt, in theory, Clive would have been better employed learning his Latin tenses with Mr Burslem, but for one who was to spend much of his life haggling with tricky Indian nawabs and others, this form of practical education may have been more useful.

But his father was not at all pleased. The Booby was not only no good at lessons but seemed to prefer the company of urchins and worse. There were complaints from local tradesmen. Richard Clive was after all a squire, even if a small one. The period might be a rough one, and the country a land of hamlets and villages without much sophistication. All the same the Booby went too far.

Richard Clive tried to discipline his battling son, but was hampered by the protection his wife gave her eldest boy. Now that he was back, he had regained the position of love a first-born usually has, without effort, with a mother. She shielded him as much as possible from the angry outbursts of her husband.

All the same, it was obvious that the boy could not be allowed to grow up in such conditions. He must be given some kind of formal education. He must be taught something, by force, if necessary. The only answer seemed to be a distant boarding school. At the age of twelve, in 1737, he was sent as a boarder to the Merchant Taylors' school in London.

The school, however, despite its strict discipline, does not seem to have been any more successful in handling Robert Clive than Daniel Bayley, Dr Eaton, the Reverend Burslem or anybody else had been. Two years later he was removed from the Merchant Taylors' school. His father would not have him at home, and he was sent instead to a small private tutorial school in Hemel Hempstead, Hertfordshire, run by a Mr Sterling, to study commerce and book-keeping. Here he appears to have remained until 1742, when, at the age of eighteen, his education was brought to an end, without, it must be admitted, any distinction.

The problem now was what to do with him? Richard Clive, although living in so remote a part of the country had, through his family, a number of connections with the City of London. As the large land-owners, such as the Dukes of Newcastle and Bedford increased their holdings, so the children of the poorer landed gentry sought in commerce the wealth that their birth had denied them. The City was the great place of opportunity. And the City was outward-looking and adventurous. It was full of companies seeking wealth, and of these City companies the most aggressive and successful was the East India Company.

It seemed almost inevitable that the unruly and adventurous Shropshire lad should join the equally unruly and adventurous Company of East Indian merchants.

In December 1742, he was offered the position of a 'writer' or clerk with the East India Company, and on 5 January 1743 was appointed to Fort St George, Madras.

Chapter 2

Reserved for Something

Trade had been carried on with the East for many centuries, for Europe was always eager to buy the spices, and especially the pepper, the East could provide. The goods used to come overland by caravan along the traditional routes that crossed Asia Minor and ended at Antioch, Alexandria and Constantinople. Here they were sold to the European buyers, to be resold in turn for the flavouring and preservation of food, and for the making of medicine.

But in the seventh century, Asia Minor was overrun by the Mohammedans. Both Alexandria and Antioch were captured, and ceased to trade with the West. Only Constantinople held out, and for the next seven centuries was the one link with the East.

In 1453 Constantinople was captured by the Turks and the last vestige of the Old Roman Empire, that Eastern Empire that Cleopatra and Mark Anthony had dreamt of establishing, vanished. The overland trade route to India was thus finally closed.

The European demand for spice and pepper still continued and alternative routes to India were sought. The Portuguese, then the best navigators in the world, led the search for a sea-route. In 1487, Bartholomew Diaz found a way round the Cape of Good Hope. Eleven years later, Vasco da Gama led an expedition, fitted out by the King of Portugal, to India; and on 20 May 1498, he moored in Calicut harbour. The route to India was open again.

The Cape of Good Hope route was not the only one the European countries tried to open. In 1492 Christopher Columbus had sailed west from Spain in order to find a route to

India that way. Expeditions were mounted by both the English and the French to find a way through the North-West Passage, but were defeated by the ice. Attempts to reopen the overland route also met with disaster.

By 1599, however, the English had emerged, after the defeat of the Spanish Armada in 1588, as the strongest maritime nation. English merchants, thanks to naval supremacy, could now force their way through hostile seas.

On 21 September 1599, one hundred and one City of London merchants put up £30,133. 6s. 8d. in order to fit out a ship to sail to India and bring back a cargo of goods. The minimum stake was £200. The maximum £3,000. The list was headed by the Lord Mayor, Sir Stephen Soame, who invested £200.

This was a normal practice. Each 'adventurer' would have a share in the profits, when the ship returned and the goods were sold, in proportion to the money he put up. Of course, if the ship was lost, sunk, captured by pirates or the enemy, all was lost. But then most of the merchants had shares in many ventures and thus spread their capital outlay.

Nevertheless, it was literally a question of 'When my ship comes home . . . ,' and if a ship had to fight its way through, that was all part of the risk.

But first permission had to be obtained from Queen Elizabeth I. As she and her advisors were trying to make peace with Spain at the time, it was considered undiplomatic to allow English merchant ships to run the risk of interception by the Spaniards.

However, by the following year, conditions were peaceful enough for the Queen to grant the 'adventurers' their request; and on 31 December 1600 they received their Charter. The East India Company had come into existence.

Four ships, the *Great Susan,* the *Hector,* the *Assention* and the *Red Dragon* were purchased and equipped, and sailed for the East as soon as possible.

The Dutch were the great rivals, and the Government was most anxious that they should be beaten in the race back to

England with the goods, especially pepper, which fetched such a high price.

But for more than two years nothing was heard of the little fleet. In the meantime, other ships were being fitted out for further expeditions.

Then, on 6 June 1603, news was received from a Frenchman that the first of the ships, the *Assention,* had safely reached European waters. She moored in the Thames ten days later, on 16 June 1603.

Guards, chosen from among the East India Company men themselves, were put on the ship. Fifty special canvas bags were sewn together to hold the precious pepper, and six suits of canvas doublet and hose, *without pockets,* were given to the six porters (or dockers) employed in filling the sacks with the pepper on board. The 'adventurers' were taking no risks. They had waited long enough for their ship to come home, and they were not going to lose a peck or corn of pepper now.

The Company expanded and acquired headquarters in the City. The somewhat loose arrangements of independent merchantmen putting up sums of money was replaced by a more stable organisation. Two main operating bodies, or Courts, as they were called, were formed. The first was the Court of Directors. This was the equivalent of the Managing Director and Board of today and was responsible for the actual running of the business, the fitting out of ships, the engagement of staff, and the control of financial policy.

The second was the Court of Proprietors. It consisted of the shareholders who had put the money into the East India Company. It had no direct executive power, but because it controlled the finance of the Company, it could, at times, and did, exercise considerable pressure on the Court of Directors.

By the time Clive sailed for India in 1743 the East India Company had been in existence for 150 years. Though he himself had no special knowledge of India, the Company was well known enough as the means for young men like him to make a fortune in the East, or die in the attempt.

It was by now powerful enough to own its own fleet of ships, or East Indiamen, as they were called. These were merchant vessels, with large spreads of sail. They were often armed and could, and did, defend themselves when attacked either by pirates or the vessels of unfriendly nations.

But because sailing ships depended on prevailing winds, the journey to the East consisted initially of sailing south-west across the Atlantic, with the help of the Trade Winds, to Rio de Janeiro in Brazil, then south-east again, across the South Atlantic to the Cape of Good Hope, round the base of Africa, and then up across the Indian Ocean to India herself.

Clive sailed from the Medway on board the East Indiaman *Winchester* on 10 March 1743. But the ship had to be refitted in Brazil. He was held up for nine whole months in Rio de Janeiro, with nothing to do but wait for his ship to resume its journey. The small amount of money his father had given him to cover the journey was soon used up. He started borrowing from the ship's captain, a man who had saved his life by throwing a bucket, with a rope tied to it, when Clive had fallen overboard in rough seas off Brazil. Clive records ruefully to his father, in his first letter home, that he lost 'the Shoes off my Feet, and with them my Silver Buckles, also a Hat and Wigg.'

It is true that Clive learnt a little Portuguese while he was in Brazil, but he does not appear to have been any more adept at learning languages than at any academic subject. Apart from this smattering of Portuguese, he relied throughout his career entirely on English and the help of interpreters.

The ship sailed on at last to Cape Town, where there was a further delay, before sailing for India. It was not until late in 1744, eighteen months after leaving England, that Clive, now heavily in debt to the ship's captain, finally disembarked at Madras. The final frustration was yet to come: his one letter of introduction to a member of the Madras community was useless. The would-be recipient had returned to England.

Madras was the main English settlement on the Coromandel, or east coast of Southern India. It had been granted to the East India Company a hundred years earlier by the Great Mogul.

The history of India is extremely complex, but for the period in question it is essential to understand that whereas the people of the various Indian States were mainly Hindu, the rulers at Delhi and elsewhere were Mohammedan. Thus the difference between the two races were those of conqueror and conquered as well as of religion, character and physique.

The Mohammedan rulers had divided India into a number of semi-independent States, or, in some cases, had taken over existing States. Each of these large States was ruled by a Mohammedan viceroy who was directly responsible to the Great Mogul in Delhi. The viceregal States were themselves quite often subdivided into smaller States, responsible to the immediate viceroy. Thus there was a three-tier system, which operated satisfactorily as long as the central command at Delhi was strong.

From 1556 to 1707 four great Mogul emperors followed one after the other. There was Akbar, a contemporary of Queen Elizabeth I. He was followed by Jehangir, Shah Jehan and finally Aurung-Zebe.

During this period, the Mogul control over the various Indian States was powerful and complete. Foreign traders were allowed to establish 'factories' or trading posts at various points on the coast, generally on useless and unhealthy swamps or on barren stretches of sand. An agreed rent was charged. The position of the trader was that of any tenant, allowed to enjoy the amenities, such as they might be, of the area, and to go about his business.

The Mogul emperors never understood the importance of sea-power; and the establishment of foreign trading posts seemed no more important than the letting of a bazaar stall to a Hindu merchant. The safety of the settlements were guaranteed by the Mogul power, and as often as not the Moguls used the European sea-power as a convenient means of travelling from one part of the coast to another. There was a considerable interchange of social life between the European merchants and the local rulers, inter-marriage was frequent, and relations were, on the whole, good.

The first English trading settlement was established at Surat, on the west coast of India, just above the tenth parallel. Captain William Hawkins obtained permission from the Emperor Jehangir in 1608 to start a trading post on a barren bit of land some way up the Tapti river. It was not a very satisfactory arrangement. Ships had to stand out from the shore and anchor in what was known as Swally Hole. Merchandise had to be loaded and unloaded on to lighters. Surat was at the mercy both of the bureaucratic and military unreliability of the Mogul officials. Despite the promise of protection from the Mogul governor, it was sacked by marauders in 1664 and 1672, and the governor did nothing.

Luckily, in 1661, Charles II had acquired, through his marriage with Catherine of Braganza, the Portuguese harbour of Bombay. It was the usual unhealthy place, but it had a deep-water harbour, and was much more satisfactory from the trading and security point of view than Surat. The East India Company managed, with admirable business acumen, to persuade Charles II to let it to them for an annual all-in rent of ten pounds.

On the other side of India, in Bengal, the first trading station, or 'factory', had been started at Hooghli, but this was later abandoned in favour of a small village on the site of the present Calcutta. In 1690 Job Charnock, the British agent, built on the muddy and fever-ridden flats of the new site a fort, which he called Fort William. By 1700 the factories in Bengal were under the control of the President and Council of Fort William.

Eight hundred miles further south along the east coast was Madras, and another hundred miles or so further on, Cuddalore. Madras was the more important of the two, and the most important part of Madras was Fort St George. It was here that Clive was to live and work. The fort was about four hundred yards long, and a hundred yards broad. It was surrounded by a wall, with bastions. There was a gateway looking on to the strand. There were about fifty European-styled houses, warehouses and offices. There was also two churches, one Anglican, the other Roman Catholic. It was here that the English, mainly employees of the East India Company, and other Europeans lived.

It was a bleak place. The long, sandy foreshore curved away from the fort. There was no harbour. The ships lay a mile or two out to sea, and the actual landing was effected in catamarans. Sometimes, in heavy seas, the surf would roll up to the very walls of the fort itself, and the catamarans would come dancing in through the rollers. Sometimes they would overturn, throwing passengers and goods indiscriminately into the turbulent seas. At other times, the sea would be flat, oily, almost immobile under the heavy, burning sun.

Nothing grew on the coast except thin palm trees standing alone or in small groups, their meagre foliage tops almost lost against the over-heated sky. Inland, strange rocks stood up like meteorites fallen on to a barren moon. The sun shimmered over the plain, making distances difficult to judge. Only the deliberately cultivated 'garden-houses' of the richer merchants formed a welcome, if forbidden, change of colour to the burnt umber of the plain.

To the north was a large area inhabited by the richer Armenian and Indian traders, and beyond this again, a mile inland, the suburbs, over-populated, unhealthy and ill cared for. Here lived, or rather died, the greater mass of the Hindu population. Epidemics swept regularly through the town, carrying thousands away in a day. Even the Europeans, in their little toy fort beneath the protection of their flag, were not immune. Without vaccination, antibiotics or even simpler drugs, they too died quickly. Other than wait for the next ship to come in, bringing longed-for letters from home, there was nothing to do for the lonely young Clive except to keep alive and wait for the day, five years still ahead, when he could start to make some money at last.

The Coromandel Coast had two monsoons a year, one in

June, the other in September, when the clouds poured torrents onto the city and submerged everything in waist-deep swirling water. The inhabitants believed that these storms were the work of the devils, and would not go out until they were over. These strong superstitions had a practical value: it was, in fact, quite easy for the rather small Hindus to be swept away by the torrents.

Clive hated his work. He was no more than a clerk in the accounts department. He could have been doing the same in the more temperate climate of London. Instead, he had to work in the hot and over-stuffy factory office. His pay was minimal: £5 a year according to the diary and accountancy book of Fort St George. It is true that he was lodged in the Writers' Barracks, and living was cheap. Nevertheless, even making allowance for modern inflation and multiplying this sum by ten, he had not quite today's equivalent of £1 a week spending money. But none of the employees was well paid. A clerk of some years' standing received only £30 a year (£300 today) and even the Governor, Christopher Morse, was paid £200 a year (£2,000 today) plus £100 gratuity (£1,000 today).

It was the Company's policy to pay its employees overseas as little as possible. No doubt the tight-fisted directors in London reckoned that this way they could keep their overheads down to a minimum. They justified their meanness by declaring that by so doing, they encouraged a magnificent spirit of free enterprise in their employees. Indeed, it was only by trading personally [and naturally shipping the goods via the East India Company], that a man on that awful coast could exist. Thus both Company and employee gained. The snag, as far as Clive was concerned, was that he had to serve five years as a clerk before he could start trading on his own account. Five years at five pounds a year added up to twenty-five pounds in all. A not very encouraging thought.

It was said that if the climate did not kill you, and your liver could survive the onslaught of drink, drugs and bad, over-spiced food, you could after that make enough in a few years to retire to England and live the life of a country gentleman.

Young men, particularly those like Clive brought up to expect wealth and yet to be deprived of it, saw in India a chance to re-establish themselves in society.

Clive had a number of other disadvantages. He arrived heavily in debt to the rapacious sea captain of the *Winchester*. He had no private allowance from home. The small amount of money given him by his father had been absorbed by the eighteen-month journey out.

Then his appearance and manners were against him. He was short, almost squat; even in youth slightly stout. He had the dark hair and high colouring of the Celt. Only his deep brown eyes were alluring, but he hardly ever gave anyone a chance of finding out. For he was gauche, awkward, taciturn and a poor conversationalist. He had none of the 'social graces' that would have made him, a newcomer, welcomed in that hot, cramped, petty society of traders and their wives. He was short-tempered and quarrelsome. He was a man impatiently enduring a hated drudgery.

Then he was appallingly homesick.

In a letter to one of his cousins, he declared: 'I may safely say that I have not enjoyed one happy day since I left my native country. I am not acquainted with any one family in the place, and have not assurance enough to introduce myself without being asked.'

He was extremely rude on arrival to the secretary of the factory, his immediate superior. This secretary complained indignantly to the Governor of his newest recruit's behaviour. The Governor ordered Clive to apologise.

This the young man did, sulkily.

The secretary, perhaps out of a mistaken desire to be kind to the churlish young man, asked him to dinner.

Clive immediately replied with insolent arrogance: 'No, sir, the Governor did not command me to *dine* with you.'

The boredom and the homesickness grew, and he began to slide into one of those depressions that were to follow him all his life. Now, with nothing to look forward to, and perhaps exhausted by the terrible heat and the easy debauchery of Indian prostitutes, he found less and less justification for his existence.

One day, when he was alone in his room in the Writers' Barracks, he picked up his pistol, cocked it, put it to his temple and pulled the trigger.

Nothing happened.

He re-cocked the pistol, and held it once more to his head.

Again nothing happened.

The door opened. Edmund Maskelyne, a young clerk seeking, like Clive, his fortune in India but, unlike Clive, provided with a private income from his family at home, came into the room. Maskelyne was much more sophisticated and self-assured than Clive. He had fitted quite easily into his new surroundings. He had a natural popularity. Perhaps the very differences in their characters drew them to each other. Edmund Maskelyne became Robert Clive's friend, his only one.

Maskelyne asked Clive what was the matter.

Clive, who was sitting gloomily on the side of his bed, asked his friend to fire the pistol out of the window.

Somewhat mystified, Maskelyne did so.

There was a loud bang, and the ball sped through the hot Indian air.

Clive jumped off the side of his bed and shouted: 'Well, I'm reserved for something. That pistol, I have twice snapped at my own head.'

Perhaps in this bizarre event he had found the justification for his continued existence. He should, by rights, have been dead. But he wasn't. Therefore he must be reserved for some purpose. Perhaps this close contact with death had excited him, had made life more desirable. Perhaps there was something of the suicide's temperament in him, when only closeness to death can make life worth living.

These can only be conjectures. Clive himself never referred to this episode. Perhaps too much can be made of it. But whether it was for this reason, or for others, his attitude changed. He was still only nineteen. He still hated his job and, in the opinions of those who worked with him, would never be any good at it. But he was not seen any more around the tarts and the card-tables.

Instead, he accepted the invitation of the Governor of Madras to make use of his library. It was an exceptionally fine library. Christopher Morse, like his predecessors, kept it stocked with the classics and books about India. The young clerks of the Company were encouraged to study there in the evenings. Not many did. But Clive did, night after night, month after month, for the next two years, filling up, during those warm Indian nights, all the gaps in his early education. Soon the Booby was a booby no more.

Chapter 3

Ensign Clive

Then, on 14 September 1746, the ennui, the boredom and the long hours in the Company's office vanished: a French fleet under Admiral La Bourdonnais appeared off Madras, and began to bombard Fort St George. Clive was a fortnight off his twenty-first birthday.

The French had come to India eighty years before, in 1664, when the astute Colbert had founded the French East India Company. Unlike its English counterpart, it was run by the State, a fact that was to have a considerable bearing on future events. The French main trading centres were at Pondicherry, about ninety miles south of Madras, and at Chandernagore, on the Hooghli, eight hundred miles to the north, on the mouth of the Ganges, and close to Fort William. In addition to the French, the Dutch still had a station on the Hooghli at Chinsura, and the Danes had two stations, one at Tranquebar, near Madras, and the other at Serampore, near Fort William.

There was an unwritten agreement that even if the European powers were at war in Europe the various trading stations around the coast of India did not attack each other. 'No war east of the Cape of Good Hope' was the cry. This after all was only natural, since the European powers in question merely rented the land from the local ruler. In the case of both Pondicherry and Madras, the 'landlord' was Anwar-ud-Din, the Nawab, or local ruler, of the Carnatic. He in turn, at least in theory, was responsible to the Nizam of Hyderabad, or viceroy, who finally acknowledged the Great Mogul himself at Delhi as his sovereign. The squabbles of the European traders, who had been given tenant rights to small strips of land on the distant coast line, could not be allowed to degenerate into acts of aggression, any more than any landlord would happily see his property damaged by the squabbles of his tenants.

But in 1741, the war of the Austrian Succession had broken out in Europe. It was a complex struggle mainly concerned with Maria Theresa of Hapsburg's determination to keep the Austrian throne in the family. In it England and France took opposite sides, but the 'no war east of the Cape of Good Hope' understanding was expected to hold.

Then in 1742 Dupleix became the Governor of Pondicherry. He was the son of a wine-merchant, and had lived a long time in India. He had been Governor of Chandernagore in Bengal before coming to Pondicherry. He was a man of fifty at the time, small but enormously active, intelligent and ambitious. He had a liking and a genius for intrigue.

His wife, Jeanne, was a Creole, an astonishingly beautiful woman, with an equally beautiful daughter. Of all the characters assembled for the coming drama, he was the only one who, because his wife spoke a number of languages, was on really intimate terms with local rulers, a fact that was to be of inestimable help to him.

She was as ambitious and tenacious as he was, and, it was said, would not hesitate to use her daughter's attractions if it meant a gain to her husband's position.

Dupleix was the first European to see in India the possibility of creating a European-dominated empire, on the lines of the empire the French were trying to create in North America. Unlike the English, Dutch and Danish traders, who never for a moment thought in terms of political power, he thought only in such terms. Perhaps the fact that he was a State employee from the beginning inclined him to this way of thought.

His plans were helped by the fact that, since the death in 1707 of Aurung-Zebe, the Mohammedan Empire was rapidly breaking up. Aurung-Zebe's heirs at Delhi no longer had the power or means of controlling their own viceroys. State after

State, from the Himalayas down to the tip of the continent, became virtually independent. The rulers still, in theory at least, acknowledged the Mogul at Delhi as their figure-head; but this did not prevent them making war upon each other, while bands of semi-organised robbers moved almost at will, from one State to another, operating a kind of large-scale protection racket; pay up or we burn you down.

At the same time, the death of a ruler was almost immediately followed by a violent and vicious struggle between the many claimants to the throne. Any kind of adventurer, Asiatic or European, could and often did take one side or the other; and, by intrigue, assassination, guile and courage pushed his particular claimant on to the throne. Failure meant almost inevitable death, but success could bring a fabulous fortune.

Dupleix saw that he could play, for France, the same game these adventurers played for themselves. He called it, in fact, 'Le Grand Jeu' and, with the indefatigable Jeanne at his side, felt that he was on a winning streak.

There was, however, one annoying obstacle: the English trading stations on the coast. He knew that, just as in North America where the French and English had been intermittently at war for years, he would have to get rid of the English sooner or later.

The trouble was, of course, that officially he could do nothing, because of that 'no war east of the Cape of Good Hope' agreement.

However, the Carnatic was a long way from France and he had, close at hand, the services of the brilliant if erratic La Bourdonnais.

La Bourdonnais was a professional privateer, whose first interest was ransom. He was also a patriotic Frenchman. He was able, without much difficulty, to combine the two roles. The privateer was a recognised force in society. The practice reached its peak during the sixteenth century, when Elizabeth I, in order to make unofficial war on Spain, encouraged her captains to harry, for their country and their own sakes, the Spanish galleons returning from South America laden with gold. They were, in fact, patriotic pirates.

By the eighteenth century, however, the practice was on the decline. The more highly organised fleets of the European countries gave the privateer less scope. The seas were no longer so free as they used to be. The galleons had gone. Only in the less patrolled Indian Ocean could they operate. La Bourdonnais was in fact the last of the privateers. Ironically, he was also by far the best admiral operating on France's behalf.

His base was at Saint Louis, on the French island of Mauritius, then called Isle de France. Situated well to the west of Madagascar, it held a strong strategic position in the Indian Ocean.

La Bourdonnais first sailed northwards to the Bay of Bengal with a make-shift squadron of eight ships. Here he met an English squadron of four fighting ships under the command of Commodore Barnet. A somewhat indecisive action followed. But Barnet decided to retire to the Hooghli to get reinforcements before attacking La Bourdonnais again. Madras, eight hundred miles to the south, was thus left unguarded, and La Bourdonnais attacked.

Despite its name and appearance, Fort St George was far from being impregnable. It was extremely vulnerable. Its walls were flimsy and in a bad state of repair. The four bastions were wrongly sighted. Worse still, the cannons were short of ammunition. Nor were there any professional soldiers in the fort. Most of the two-hundred-strong garrison were peons. These were locally recruited mercenaries who sold whatever military expertise they had to anyone who would hire them. Many of them were criminals and vagabonds, or poor peasants who could think of nothing better to do. They were not expected to fight, but more to protect the warehouses from thieves. Whenever any fighting did break out, they tended to change sides, especially if they were on the losing side.

Finally there was nobody with any real military knowledge in command. The Governor, Christopher Morse, was a merchant. His job was to make trade, not war.

La Bourdonnais, on the other hand, had at his disposal two thousand French regular troops and trained sepoys. The sepoys were a French invention and an answer to the shortage of French troops; for the home government was never keen to denude other theatres of war. They were recruited locally like the peons but, unlike the peons, they were selected with care. The individual sepoy was given the same thorough training as the French regular soldier; so that, very soon, they equalled their European counterpart in drill, discipline and the handling of weapons.

La Bourdonnais also had the full fire-power of his fleet at his disposal. The issue was never in doubt. After a token, and somewhat ineffectual fight (the French had no losses, the English five), Morse surrendered the fort. There was nothing else he could do.

The French admiral soon made it known that he was not after prestige but ransom. A figure of thirty thousand pounds was mentioned. On the payment of this sum, he declared, the fort would be returned. Morse discussed the matter with his colleagues and, while agreeing to pay the ransom, asked for three months to collect the cash.

La Bourdonnais promptly agreed, and the 'war' for all intents and purposes came to an end. He placed the English employees on parole not to attempt to escape or take any war-like action against his troops. He then waited for the ransom to be paid.

But Dupleix, at Pondicherry, was furious when he heard of La Bourdonnais's bargain. He had no desire to see the fort returned to the Company. On the contrary, his intention was to raze it to the ground and eliminate all English influence in Madras.

A violent quarrel broke out between the two French commanders, much to the amused interest of the Company employees; but just as it seemed as if they could never agree, even to disagree, a storm broke over the scratch French squadron and did so much damage to the ships that Bourdonnais had to return to the Isle de France, leaving Dupleix in complete control of Madras.

The French Governor had no hesitation in declaring that the agreement drawn up between his admiral and the English Company was null and void, and that new and far harsher terms were to be imposed. He even had poor Christopher Morse and some of the senior members of the Company marched as prisoners, in Roman fashion, through the town of Pondicherry.

The Company employees felt that these actions released them from the parole they had given La Bourdonnais. The younger and more adventurous ones, who had looked on with anger at the feeble defence put up by the fort, immediately escaped.

Among them was Clive, disguised as a Moslem, and his friend Edmund Maskelyne.

Clive was a particularly successful Moslem. His dark swarthy features needed very few additions to give him an oriental look. A black beard was carefully stuck on round his chin. A Mohammedan turban hid his European hair, and he wore a long white gown, lent to him by his own servant.

Together, the two young men hurried out of the fort, across the arid plain, and made their way south towards Fort St David, over a hundred miles away.

The problem was that Pondicherry lay also on the coast between Fort St George and Fort St David. Here Dupleix and his army had complete control. Fort St David was only twelve miles further south. A huge detour across the boulder-strewn plain became necessary, before the escapers scrambled at last into the relative safety of Fort St David, soon to become the last English outpost in that part of India, and, for this reason, the object of Dupleix's next attack.

Fort St David, though even smaller than Fort St George, was a less arid place. Already the surrounding plain had become more fertile. There were fields of maize and rice. The villages were closer together. There were lush green gardens and all kinds of trees: mango, almond and other fruit trees. Even the inevitable palm trees by the seashore were more luxurious than those at Fort St George.

Though the fort itself was small, the European concession was large. Its size had been determined in 1690, when the Mahrattas who owned the land had agreed to cede all the area 'within ye randome shott of a piece of ordnance.' The wily Mr Hatsell, who was negotiating the deal on behalf of the East India Company, brought with him from Madras the largest gun and the best gunner. The random shot fell well beyond the nearby Indian town of Cuddalore and a number of villages that became known as 'cannonball' villages.

Within this ample space, the East India Company merchants had built their airy houses, and surrounded them with luxurious gardens. Here, behind high brick walls, were walks shaded by tulip-trees, and beds filled with pomegranates, oranges and pineapples.

To this small paradise, then, came Clive and his friend Edmund Maskelyne in their strange disguises.

In the meantime however, Anwar-ud-Din, the Nawab of the Carnatic and the real owner of Madras, had become extremely annoyed at Dupleix's high-handed actions. He knew about Dupleix's ambitions. The Carnatic stretched along almost the whole east coast of the Indian peninsular. He realised that it would be the first State to be taken over by the French. He was already having trouble to the north with the Mahrattas, a confederacy of extremely talented but piratical Hindu chiefs, whose main object in life was to plunder rival States. Neither Anwar-ud-Din's immediate superior, the Nizam of Hyderabad, nor the ever-weakening Great Mogul, hundreds of miles away in Delhi, could help him. He decided to throw the French out of Madras before they managed to make themselves too powerful.

He sent his son and ten thousand of his best cavalry against the small French force holding Madras. It seemed that nothing could save Dupleix from having, in his turn, to surrender Fort St George. But the French had two great advantages over the Indian horsemen: discipline and fire-power. As the Nawab's cavalry hurled themselves at the French, the latter did not panic or break. They waited for the right moment near St Thomé, and let the whole force of their artillery and musket fire crash into the charging cavalry. The effect was devastating. Indian cavalry had never before met such a volume of accurate unremitting fire. The charge turned to a rout. By the victory of St Thomé, the French showed for the first time, that small, disciplined, well-armed European forces could defeat far larger but undisciplined bodies of Indian troops. It was a lesson not to be lost on young Robert Clive who was just about to begin his own military career.

Escaping from Fort St George had been an exciting event. Nevertheless once arrived in Fort St David, there was the problem of how to exist. Trade was becoming rapidly restricted as the French became more and more aggressive. With Pondicherry so close, and Commodore Barnet still refitting eight hundred miles to the north, Fort St David, despite its pleasant rural aspects, was in a very precarious position. However, the Company adapted itself to the changed conditions, and John Hinde, the Governor there, took over the responsibility for the whole of the Coromandel Coast, now that Christopher Morse was a prisoner of the French. The escaped clerks from Madras were taken on to the already over-staffed books of St David.

There was little to do except wait for the French to attack. Christopher Morse's library had gone. Clive joined in gambling with the rest.

One day Clive lost money to an officer who had a reputation of cheating at cards. A number of the young clerks had already lost money they could not afford. None, however, had dared challenge the officer but had paid up.

When it came to his turn to pay, Clive refused to do so, saying that he did not pay cheats. The officer immediately challenged Clive to a duel. Duelling was not permitted officially, but continued to be practised unofficially all the same. Clive accepted the challenge. He fired first and missed.

The officer came up to the young man, and holding the pistol to his head, ordered Clive to beg for his life.

Clive did so immediately.

Following up his advantage, the officer now ordered that Clive should retract his allegations concerning the play.

Clive shook with fury. It was all right asking for his life to be spared, but he would not change his opinions. That was, to him, a question of principle.

'Fire and be damned,' he shouted, 'I said you cheated. I say so still. I will never pay you.'

The officer looked at him in astonishment, hesitated and then put away his pistol, muttering; 'You're mad.'

Clive became the hero of the young clerks. He was the only one who had stood up to the cheat. An attempt was made to get the officer brought to court. Clive was asked to give evidence, but he refused to testify against his erstwhile enemy, saying; 'He has given me my life, and, though I am resolved on never paying money which was unfairly won, or again associating with him, I shall never do him an injury.'

There were, however, other fights to keep him busy. The French, under the command of Captain Paradis, who had been the victor against the Nawab at St Thomé, now attacked the fort.

Fort St David was stronger than Fort St George; and the town of Cuddalore, situated about a mile to the south, was fortified on three of its sides by a wall flanked with bastions. It was open to the sea but here a sand-bar thrown up by the breaking waves formed an effective barrier.

The English now knew that if Fort St David were captured, the Company's influence in this part of India would disappear, probably for ever. They knew too that their own fate would be that of prisoners of the French. Finally, although there was no sign of a British squadron out at sea, there was no sign of a French one either, La Bourdonnais indeed was destined never to return to the Coromandel

Coast. He was to be recalled to France and, largely because of Dupleix's violent denunciations, was to face unmerited imprisonment in the Bastille on a criminal charge of treason because of his so-called trading with the enemy. Although he was acquitted and released, he died in disgrace. He was probably the finest potential officer the French had, but like so many of his contemporaries was destroyed by his own country.

Although the French commander Paradis had a ten-to-one superiority over the English, he too had his problems, the main one being the presence of Anwar-ud-Din, the Nawab of the Carnatic, and his two sons with a number of troops. They had come in support of the English. The Nawab's move had been due to a number of factors. He was expected, by treaty, to come to the assistance of the English if they were attacked. But that did not weigh heavily with him. He had not come to their assistance when Fort St George was being pounded. More potent was the order from his superior, the Nizam of Hyderabad, now also alarmed by Dupleix's duplicity and ambition, to take action. Finally he wanted very much to avenge his son's defeat at St Thomé.

A good deal of indecisive fighting, double-crossing and attempts to buy off the Nawab's forces continued from December 1746 to March 1747; but, despite all attacks, the French were not able to capture Fort St David. One of the reasons for this failure was undoubtedly the presence and, in particular, the aggressive activity of young Clive. Although not then an official soldier, he was always to be seen where the fighting was heaviest, and was ready to lead a counter-attack wherever necessary.

As a result, the Governor of Fort St David, in a general letter dated 2 May 1747, wrote as follows to the Directors in London:

'Mr Robert Clive writer in the service being of a Martial Disposition, and having acted as a Volunteer in Our Late Engagements, we have Granted him an Ensign's Commission, upon his Application for the same.'

Now at last Clive was no longer a despised clerk, sitting in a stuffy office entering details of bills of lading. He was an ensign in the Company's service leading an active and dangerous life. He was aware too of the utmost importance at this moment of keeping Fort St David in English hands. Finally, on the practical side, his pay as an ensign was double that of a clerk.

So the year 1747 passed, the garrison of Fort St David foiling rather than defeating two French attacks, and living in permanent expectation of a new and much heavier attack as soon as Dupleix and his scheming wife could really neutralise the Nawab of the Carnatic and receive sufficient reinforcements from France to make success inevitable. But with the war of the Austrian Succession still dragging on, Louis XV's Government was not too eager to send troops to India. It did not share, to the same degree, Dupleix's vision of a great new empire in the East. Besides, it needed its troops in other, more important, battle areas. There were the French armies to be maintained on the mainland of Europe, in America and at bases such as Mauritius (Isle de France). Indeed the Coromandel Coast was, both to the English and the French at that time, a minor sphere of activity, fought on the one hand by a French governor largely deprived of the necessary troops and an English trading company almost totally unsupported by the home Government. The really decisive battles of the war were being fought elsewhere.

In January 1748, Major Stringer Lawrence landed at Fort St David. He had been engaged as early as December 1746 by the Directors of the East India Company to replace Major Knipe, the commander at Fort St George who had died in May 1743. It had taken the Directors three years to find a suitable replacement. Stringer Lawrence was forty-nine. He had served at Fontenoy and Culloden and retired from Major-General Clayton's regiment (subsequently the West Yorkshire Regiment) on taking service with the East India Company.

The record of the Directors' Proceedings for 17 December

1746 read:

'Resolved that the garrison of Fort St George be strengthened with a number of recruits, sergeants and ensigns, and that an able officer be sent from hence, as Major thereof, at the salary of £250 per annum and one hundred guineas for his charges out.'

Major Stringer Lawrence sailed with a hundred and fifty men, in the *Winchelsea* on 18 February 1747. The journey took eleven months. At Cape Town news of the capture of Madras was received, whereupon the ship sailed, in order probably to avoid La Bourdonnais's attention, first to Batavia in the Dutch East Indies, before turning back in a wide sweep to the Coromandel Coast.

Stringer Lawrence was, *par excellence,* a regimental officer. Honest, hard-working and conscientious, he could inspire great confidence even in inferior troops. Macaulay describes him as 'gifted with no intellectual faculty higher than plain good sense' but, in fact, most of the fighting he conducted was of the tactical, that is to say local, rather than strategical, or world-embracing kind. He was Clive's first real military commander.

He was the right man, at the right moment for the right job. He showed this immediately on his arrival at Fort St David. Taking command of the enthusiastic if somewhat amateur defenders, he immediately organised them into companies, each consisting of a captain, a lieutenant, an ensign, four sergeants, four corporals, three drummers and seventy privates. He set up a camp outside the walls of the fort for better safety, and soon uncovered a plot whereby the peons, who were in secret negotiations with Dupleix, would desert to the French. That eager new ensign Robert Clive was assigned to one of the new companies.

Stringer Lawrence had been barely six months at Fort St David, when the French attacked again. Eight hundred Europeans and a thousand Indian troops made a forced march from Pondicherry and appeared on the morning of 17 June 1748, three miles from Cuddalore. Stringer Lawrence, who had been warned of this attack, showed his tactical grasp by immediately withdrawing to the fort, and letting it be known that he did not consider Cuddalore tenable. As soon as night fell however he marched back to the Cuddalore ramparts with every man and gun he could find. So that when, at midnight, the French started moving cautiously forward, they were met with such violent and unexpected fire that they fled back to Pondicherry; and Dupleix, brilliant politician but no general, gave up the idea of capturing Fort St David, and thought instead of other ways of getting rid of the East India Company. Thanks to Stringer Lawrence's leadership and effectiveness, Fort St David and the Company were no longer in direct danger.

But at this moment there appeared, unfortunately, the unlikely figure of Admiral Boscawen to take over command of the land forces from Stringer Lawrence. The fall of Madras had at last brought the English Government's attention to this part of the global struggle with France, and when the Directors of the East India Company asked for official help, Admiral Boscawen was eventually sent out from England with a fleet of some 20 ships and 1,400 regular troops, including artillery.

Admirals may be all right on the sea, but are rarely so on land. Boscawen was no exception. He lost time trying, unsuccessfully, to capture Isle de France (Mauritius) on his way to India, but, when he did reach Fort St David on 29 July 1748, resolved immediately to march on Pondicherry and attempt to dislodge, in his turn, the French from their stronghold.

The troops were landed and by 8 August 1748 some 3,720 Europeans, including sailors, soldiers and a Dutch contingent from Negapatam, moved towards Pondicherry. It did not achieve anything except the loss of 1,065 men, the useless expenditure of an enormous amount of ammunition, and the capture by the French of stout-hearted Stringer Lawrence who, when a contingent of panicky sailors fled before a sudden charge, refused to move. As the historian Orme was to remark later: 'There are very few instances of late years of a siege carried on by the English with less skill than this of Pondicherry.'

It gave that newly-appointed young ensign Clive his first experience of active service in the field. Until then he had hopped about, courageously but in an unprofessional way, around the ramparts of forts and in their near vicinity. Now he was a part of a professional army, engaged upon a definite campaign. It seemed to those who were with him that he was everywhere at the same time, always volunteering for the most dangerous missions, often acting on the spur of the moment.

This, on one occasion at least, brought him trouble of an unexpected kind.

He was in charge of a battery that was running short of ammunition. Instead of ordering one of his men to fetch a new supply, he ran back himself. One of the regular officers, perhaps jealous of the notoriety this amateur ensign had already gained, said sneeringly to his companions that Clive was running away.

Clive demanded an apology. When this was not given, he challenged the officer to a duel, but the latter, feeling perhaps that it was below his dignity to fight with an upstart ensign, merely cuffed the young man as if he were a boy.

Clive immediately drew his sword, and would have started to fight then and there had not both he and his opponent been immediately put under open arrest for illegal duelling.

At the subsequent court of inquiry, the officer who had insulted Clive was ordered to apologise in front of the whole regiment. This he did, and the next day resigned his commission.

Soon Clive's name was known to the whole of the force as a man of extraordinary bravery, of great activity, but also one it was dangerous to insult.

But now, outside events were to take control. News of the signing of the Treaty of Aix-la-Chapelle reached the two sides in November 1748. The war of the Austrian Succession was over at last. Hostilities, at least for the time being, ceased, and Major Stringer Lawrence was allowed to return to Fort St David, on parole, pending ratification of the treaty.

Chapter 4

Dupleix's Duplicity

Dupleix was not at all pleased that his Government had signed the treaty, as it meant that he had, very reluctantly, to hand Madras back to the East India Company.

The Treaty of Aix-La-Chapelle covered other theatres than India. One was North America. Here the French had established posts and settlements from Louisburg, on Cape Breton Island to the north, along the St Lawrence, the Great Lakes, the Ohio and the Mississippi. They formed a defensive chain that contained the thirteen colonies, and prevented the largely English and Dutch colonists from expanding westwards.

In the recent fighting, France had lost Louisburg. Now, with the signing of peace, she agreed to give back Madras in India for the return of Louisburg. For despite all Dupleix could say, the French Government placed a higher priority on their American than on their Indian achievements.

Nor was Admiral Boscawen pleased at the outbreak of peace. He had come all this way to India to bring home a victory. He had been baulked at Mauritius and at Pondicherry. Now this unfortunate treaty looked like depriving him of his last chance. This might well have been the case in the more regulated European waters, but India was a long way from home; and, in the state of internal chaos of the country, everything was possible. The problem was how to bring back a victory without actually declaring war on anybody.

An opportunity soon occurred. For some time a prince by the name of Sahojee had been living under the protection of the Company. He was a pretender to the throne of Tanjore, a small State immediately to the south of Fort St David. He claimed that the people of Tanjore disliked the present ruler, his brother needless to say, and would rise up in rebellion as soon as he, Sahojee, appeared at the border. As a reward for English assistance, Sahojee promised to give the East India Company Devicotah on the Coleroon river, some twenty miles from Fort St David.

A first expedition in March 1749 of four hundred and thirty Europeans and a thousand European-trained Indian troops, of 'sepoys', as they were first called, marched under Captain Cope's command to Devicotah, but, owing to lack of supplies, returned almost at once to Fort St David. In the fort's cash book the following laconic but revealing entry is recorded: 'By Expedition to Tanjore, Paid Sundry Persons for the losses of Provisions etc which they carried for the use of the Army upon the first Expedition thither, and which when they retreated was Part of it taken by the Enemy and part lost in the River . . . £245. 0 0.'

The only positive result of this abortive expedition was to show the East India Company that Sahojee's claims to popularity were somewhat exaggerated. Not a single Tanjorean had risen in his support during the whole episode.

A second expedition was sent out, this time under the command of Stringer Lawrence himself. Clive was by now a lieutenant.

As soon as Stringer Lawrence's artillery had breached the walls of Devicotah, Clive volunteered to lead the assault party. Lawrence agreed. Clive, at the head of thirty-five English and seven hundred Indian soldiers, charged forward.

Unknown to the English, however, the Indian troops held back and soon the small band of Englishmen was alone. At this moment, Tanjorean horsemen first encircled and then attacked them. In a few minutes all but four of the Englishmen were killed. Clive himself narrowly avoided death by side-stepping a charging Tanjorean cavalryman. With the three other survivors he managed to regain the English lines, and even to take part in the final, and this time, successful assault on Devicotah.

The incumbent Tanjore ruler was only too pleased to make peace. He ceded Devicotah to the East India Company, thus making his usurping brother's promise useless. The Company's soldiers returned to Fort St David; and Sahojee was once again pensioned off.

Admiral Boscawen's orders included the taking over, when the French were ready to honour their treaty obligations, of Madras. The dismantling of French installations took longer than expected. He finally sailed for the town on 18 August 1749. On 3 September, the Governor of Fort St David was able to tell the Board in London: 'We have now the Satisfaction to Acquaint you that Madras is again in our possession in which place Genl Boscawen enter'd the 21st Ult° when the French Troops Evacuated it.'

Two months later Admiral Boscawen was on his way home, his glory and his victory in his pocket.

The small Devicotah affair had an importance far above its reality. It was the first time that the East India Company had acted in an aggressive way, rather than, as before, in self-defence. It was the first time it had acquired territory through attack. It also brought Clive prominently to Stringer Lawrence's notice. From now onwards there was no question that Clive was a civilian volunteer pretending to be an officer. In Stringer Lawrence's opinion, Clive was one of those rare people: a natural soldier. He reported to the Directors of the Company that they had found in Clive a potential military genius.

However, in the meantime, it was back to the office stool in Madras for the exuberant young officer. The Company allowed him the position he would have reached, had he not left. And through Stringer Lawrence's insistence, he was put in charge of the providing of supplies to the European troops.

This meant that there was, at last, a considerable improvement in his financial state. He was no longer so hard up. He could allow himself a few modest luxuries.

Nevertheless, with peace and stability came the depressions that always seemed to attack him when his life was not in danger. The depression brought on a nervous fever. He complained that his stomach felt as hard as wood. His liver, weakened by his childhood illness, did not function properly. He was subject to bilious attacks that left him irritable and exhausted. Even at this early age, gallstones, from which he was to suffer so much later, seem to have formed and could be dispersed only by taking drugs. Opium was his favourite means of relieving the pain. He began to take more and more of it.

He tried to fight both the depression and the pain; but each led to the other. The nervous contraction of his stomach did not help the badly functioning liver. His excessive bile increased the tension in his stomach. With little to take his mind off his physical and mental condition, he became increasingly morose and difficult.

In the end, there was nothing for it but to take time off from work and to go on holiday. So, in the cool season of 1750, he went north on a long cruise in the Bay of Bengal, and took the opportunity of visiting Calcutta.

Ever since he had left England, seven years earlier, he had always been drawn to Calcutta and the Bengal. He had written home to his father, asking whether he could not be transferred there.

Unlike Madras with its bleak plain, Calcutta, situated seventy miles up the Hooghli river, was surrounded by a lush and fertile land. Here, among Bengal's bright green rice-fields, were foreign settlements, English, French, Dutch and Danish, far more prosperous than those of Madras. Here were cities, opulent with wealth and eastern ostentation, and thousands of busy villages dotted across the great productive plain. Bengal was the most fertile and wealthiest of the Indian states, and though Calcutta was not the official capital, it was the financial capital.

There was the usual fort, this time called Fort William, where the Governor lived in a fine Georgian house. An artificial lake had been built behind the fort. Around it were the great mansions of the wealthy foreign merchants. Tree-shaded walks led from house to house, and down to the navigable river itself.

Around the settlement a large ditch had been dug some years earlier when it seemed as if the Mahrattas, the marauding Hindu horsemen from central India, would attack Calcutta. The ditch was still there, but now unused, a dumping ground, swarming with malaria-carrying mosquitoes. So that this rich and eastern paradise was surrounded by a foetid swamp, the means of its own destruction. Thousands of Europeans, unused to the violent fevers and unprotected by any form of inoculation, fell sick, retired first to the hospital beyond the fort, and then, as often as not, to the cemetery beyond.

To Clive, however, recuperating from his private nervous disorders, Calcutta was a gentle relaxing place. He would go riding in the mornings, and then, although still no society darling, would mingle in conversation with other of his compatriots, or attend evening parties at the large houses. He spent many hours writing letters home. Soon his health improved, he could cut down on the drug-taking, and he could return to Madras, refreshed, invigorated and ready for the next adventure.

It was soon to come.

By 1750 Dupleix's cunning manoeuvring had brought off a stupendous double coup: nominees of his took over both Hyderabad and the Carnatic.

Of the two, the most impressive was undoubtedly Hyderabad.

In 1724, Asaf Jah, Nizam-ul-Mulk, had left Delhi in disgust and moved to the Deccan, which means South, and in this huge central Indian area had created the state of Hyderabad. Here, as Nizam of Hyderabad, he had ruled as Soubahdar, or viceroy of the emperor, for twenty-four years until his own death in 1748.

Among the self-ruling States under his jurisdiction was the Carnatic. The following year, 1749, Anwar-ud-Din, the Nawab of the Carnatic whose armies had been as ineffective against the French at Madras as in support of the English at Fort St David, was killed in battle.

Thus the two key positions in southern India became vacant at more or less the same time. The usual in-fighting between rival claimants broke out; and, as a result of Dupleix's activities, one nominee, Muzzaffar Jang was appointed Nizam of Hyderabad, and his other, Chunda Sahib, Nawab of the Carnatic.

The installation of the new Nizam was a magnificent occasion. It took place at Pondicherry and the star was undoubtedly Dupleix himself. Dressed in a Mohammedan robe more splendid that the Nizam's, he sat in the place of greatest honour. No one had ever seen a foreigner so honoured. The new Nizam in a fit of generosity, no doubt suggested by Dupleix himself, gave the French control over the whole of India south of the Kistna river, an area that extended six hundred miles from north to south, and at its largest was five hundred miles in width, the size, in fact, of France. Thirty million people lived there.

The elated Dupleix had an enormous monument erected to himself, telling in French, Hindustani, Persian and Malabar of his successes; and founded near to it, the town of Dupleix-Fatihabad, the place of Dupleix's victory.

The newly-appointed Nizam of Hyderabad was assassinated a few weeks later, on his way home, but de Bussy, Dupleix's brilliant general, readily found an alternative Nizam; and, once installed at Hyderabad, made quite certain that French influence was paramount.

In the meantime, the installation of Chunda Sahib to the lesser but still vital throne of the Carnatic was equally successful. His real name was Hussein Dost Cawn. He had had a somewhat turbulent career having, until Dupleix ransomed him, been a prisoner of the Mahrattas. The name Chunda Sahib was given him by his enemies, as a sign of contempt: Chunda meaning servant. However by 1750 all that was forgotten. The great Imperial Palace at Arcot was his, so was the whole of the Coromandel Coast, at, of course, the discretion of the French.

The English, meanwhile, made no progress. They were still being restricted to the immediate vicinity of Forts St George and St David. It is true that they still had a nominee for the nawabship of the Carnatic (their candidate for the greater prize of Nizam of Hyderabad had been killed) in the person of Mohammed Ali, a son of Anwar-ud-Din. But this was of little comfort to the English for Mohammed Ali was besieged at Trichinopoly, over two hundred miles south of Madras, by Chunda Sahib himself.

Robert Clive continued his dual role of merchant and military man.

In a general letter to the Company, dated 12 February 1750, the Governor and Council announced: 'Mr Robert Clive who has acted in a Military Capacity ever since the Capture of Fort St George having desired to be permitted to resume his station as Covenanted Servant, we have appointed him stewart here in room of Mr Smith. . . .'

It was an exacting and responsible position, since it meant provisioning the garrison at Fort St David. Although Fort St George had been handed back to the East India Company, Fort St David continued to be the headquarters of the Company for over another year until, in fact, 23 August 1751, when Fort St George again became the Company's leading factory.

Clive was responsible too for the accountancy and financial details of the Commissary. Quite large sums passed through his hands. The Fort St David cash book records the following: '9 July 1750: By Robert Clive Stewart advanced him to provide provisions for the Garrison: £2285. 2(5).'

In September, he got £1,000 and in October a further £1,300.

Every penny of these sums had to be accounted for, and this experience in the Quartermaster side of military life was to be of considerable usefulness to him later. It also allowed him to take part in any campaign that might be going, to an even closer degree, perhaps, than his friend Edmund Maskelyne, who had at the same time volunteered to serve solely as a soldier.

Clive thus took part in a quasi-civilian capacity in what became known as 'the disgraceful affair at Volconda' when Captain de Gingen, a Swiss in the Company's pay, courageous but not sagacious, attempted to relieve Trichinopoly by investing Volconda, but was himself forced to retreat hastily, after his troops had panicked and run into Trichinopoly. Clive managed to get back to Fort St David.

The trouble was that with Stringer Lawrence's return to England on sick leave, soon after being released by the French, there was no one with sufficient military knowledge to take over command. Though Stringer Lawrence believed in Clive's potentialities, the latter, by the very nature of his responsibilities, was specifically forbidden to take part in any fighting. Besides, although his bravery was acknowledged, few besides Lawrence believed in his genius. Thus the only possible military commander was, at this difficult time, unable to use his gifts.

However, Thomas Saunders, a dour, hard but clearheaded man, had taken over as Governor of Fort St David. In July 1751 Saunders sent one of the members of the Council, George Pigot, to Trichinopoly with instructions to get through with reinforcements and supplies. Clive volunteered to accompany the party, pointing out that it was his responsibility to see that all garrisons were supplied. Saunders agreed.

The convoy of troops and supplies covered the hundred miles through the hot Indian countryside, brushed aside French scouting forces and under cover of darkness managed to reach Trichinopoly safely. Here Cope and de Gingen received both the slender reinforcements and more abundant supplies gratefully.

Clive, looking at the huge rock-fortress that towered above the Indian houses by the river, came to two important tactical conclusions. The first was that, given supplies, Trichinopoly could hold out for some time yet, but not for ever; the second that, given the distance from Fort St David, and the even further distance from Fort St George, the strength of Chunda Sahib's besieging army and the weakness of the English forces, it could not, at present, be relieved by direct attack.

The problem was what to do. If Trichinopoly fell, it would be the end of the East India Company's continued existence on the Coromandel Coast. For it would not be long before Chunda Sahib, encouraged and led by Dupleix, found both the excuse and the strength to oust, once and for all, the English out of Forts St David and St George. Only if the pro-English Mohammed Ali could be released and put on the Carnatic throne would the Company be safe.

Pigot and Clive with twelve sepoys turned back for Fort St David. Travelling fast on horseback they hoped to avoid a clash with the French and Chunda Sahib's troops.

They managed to do this, but had not counted on the Poligars, free-lance robbers and bandits who pillaged wherever they could. Continuously attacked, much in the same way that a wagon-train might be attacked by Red Indians on its way, in the next century, across the plains of America, the party owed their escape to the fleetness of their horses. As it was, of the twelve sepoys, seven were killed, and only Clive, Pigot and five sepoys made Fort St David.

Clive went straight to Thomas Saunders and told him about the situation at Trichinopoly. It was then that he put forward a plan that had been in his mind ever since he had left the fort.

It was this: since it was impossible, with the resources available, to relieve Trichinoply, perhaps an attack on an area sensitive to Chunda Sahib would force him to divert troops and thus relieve the pressure on the besieged fortress.

Possibly. But where?

Clive suggested an attack on Arcot, the capital of the Carnatic, and the place where Chunda Sahib's newly-acquired palace was situated. Arcot was seventy miles from Madras, whereas Trichinopoly was over two hundred. It was lightly held while Chunda Sahib's main army was away. Arcot held the strategic solution to the problem.

Thomas Saunders agreed. Perhaps he had some of Stringer Lawrence's confidence in the twenty-five-year-old Captain, or perhaps he realised that the plan, hazardous though it might be, was the only hope they had.

In all events, he put Clive on board the *Wager* and sent him up the coast by sea past Pondicherry to Madras, carrying with him a letter to the Deputy-Governor at Fort St George, telling the latter that the reason for Clive's visit would be communicated to him.

Thomas Saunders was taking no chances. The success of Clive's plan depended on secrecy. If Chunda Sahib heard that any kind of expedition was being mounted against his capital, he would immediately make sure that the defenders were warned – and strengthened. So nothing was to be in writing. Everything was to be kept between the Governor, Clive and the Deputy-Governor. Even the main body of the Council was not to be informed. One slip of the tongue in that land of spies and counter spies, bribery and intrigue could wreck the whole plan.

Clive reached Fort St George on 23 August 1751, and a few days later the following laconic entry was recorded in the fort's Diary and Consultation Book: 'March'd out a Detachment under command of Captain Clive.'

The detachment consisted of two hundred Europeans and three hundred sepoys. There were eight officers, six of whom had never been in action before. Four of the latter were young clerks in the East India Company's service who, inspired by Clive's example, had volunteered for service. Clive had exactly three field-guns. It was all that could be spared. As it was, Fort St David was left with only a hundred defenders and Fort St George with fifty. A considerable risk, considering that Pondicherry, Dupleix's headquarters twelve miles from Fort St David, cut direct communications between the two forts.

The Carnatic was almost as big as England. Its inland

capital of Arcot was over a hundred miles up the Palar river, but by marching south-west out of Fort St George, the distance was reduced to seventy. The country was wild. There were potential enemies everywhere. It was as if five hundred foreigners set off from Oxford on a thundery day to capture London.

In addition, Clive was marching through a country of which he was technically a guest, in support of a 'usurper', for that was how Mohammed Ali would appear, besieged two hundred miles away to the south by the 'loyal' troops. The political dangers were as great as the military and climatic ones. If it were not that the East India Company was fighting for its trading posts on the Coromandel Coast, Clive would never have considered setting off on this expedition, for unlike Dupleix neither he nor the Company directors in London had any imperial ambitions. Indeed, the East India Company's officials had, until the arrival of Dupleix, been extremely careful to remain on amicable terms with their landlords.

But since the signing of the Treaty of Aix-la-Chapelle, the old patterns were changing once and for all. Clive's first steps from Fort St George set off events far greater than he or any one else could imagine.

Chapter 5

Arcot

It was 26 August 1751 when Clive marched out of Fort St George. It was extremely hot and humid, half-way between two monsoons. There was thunder in the air. It took them three days hard marching to reach Conjeveram on the Palar river. Arcot was another thirty miles upstream.

Here, in the pleasant riverside town with its large pagoda, Clive received the first definite news of the strength of the Arcot garrison. It was eleven hundred, double his attacking force. The odds were acceptable, but Clive felt it prudent to add to the feeble strength of his artillery in case the walls of Arcot needed breaching. He sent an urgent message back to Madras asking for two eighteen-pounder guns to be sent to him.

Then, without waiting, he marched on. Almost at once an enormous storm burst on his mini-army. The rain poured down amid almost constant thunder and lightning. It was enough to make the toughest hesitate and take shelter. The sepoys, believing that the gods and devils were at work, were scared and ready to run.

But Clive, always aware that he should get to Arcot before Chunda Sahib, marched on regardless of the thunder and lightning, the bleak torrential rain.

The sepoys, new to this kind of European drive and determination, began to look upon Clive as somebody outside the normal human range, perhaps himself a god, for who other than a god would dare to defy the gods themselves?

This belief was also shared by the local inhabitants who, crouching in their shelters from the storm, saw, almost with disbelief, the five hundred men led by their stocky inexhaustible commander march straight through the storm as if it did not even exist.

Rumour rushed ahead of the advancing troops. The eleven hundred indolent defenders of Arcot heard that the Devil himself was heading their way, and that not even the thunderbolts of the gods could stop the advance. If, they reckoned with Eastern logic, thunderbolts were useless against Clive, what possible use could they be? The whole garrison prudently vanished as Clive marched into the city.

The town itself was not defended, the fort standing on its own with the houses around it. A huge crowd, estimated at a hundred thousand, turned out to watch in awe this small band of men march through the streets.

Within a few hours of arriving at Arcot, Clive entered the fort. Not a shot had been fired, nor were there any casualties.

He wasted no time. This was only the opening move in his plan. By his quick and decisive action he had reached Arcot before Chunda Sahib or the defenders could do anything. It would not be long now before the reaction of both would be violent.

His first act was to make sure that the population came over to his side, or at least remained neutral. There were fifty thousand pounds' worth of goods belonging to the Arcot merchants locked up for safe-keeping in the fort. These were immediately handed over to their owners. In addition there were three to four thousand people living in the fort itself. These were allowed to remain. Strict orders were issued to the troops to refrain from looting and rape. These instructions were almost as unbelievable to the inhabitants as Clive's march had been to the defenders. The leading citizens came over to Clive. There would be no trouble from that side.

He then set about strengthening the fort. It was not in a very good condition. There was a mile of rambling walls; many of them needed repairing. The ramparts were narrow and unsuitable for artillery. The parapets were too low and thin-skinned. Many of the towers were half-ruined. None would stand up to determined artillery fire. There was a ditch, or moat, around the fort, but it was clogged and semi-dry. The ten-foot fausse-braye between the moat and the walls of the fort had no parapet by the edge of the ditch, so could not be used by the defenders to shoot down anyone fording or forcing the moat.

The two gates leading into the fort, one on the north-west side, the other on the east, had no drawbridges. Instead, a causeway crossed the ditch. Though the gateways were themselves bastions protruding forty feet from the main walls of the fort, they were overlooked by the nearby houses. Attempts to burn down these houses failed, as they were made of stone and had very little wood.

However, the garrison repaired as much as they could. On the credit side was the discovery that the fort was well supplied with ammunition, and had in addition eight pieces of artillery, ranging from four to eight-pounders.

Although busy on the fort, Clive had not forgotten the eleven hundred erstwhile defenders who had disappeared on his arrival. They would, he realised, soon recover from their superstitious fear and, driven on by a need to rehabilitate themselves both in their own and more importantly in Chunda Sahib's estimation, return. So he decided to sally out in search of them. It was anyhow a wise decision. Attack is the best means of defence. A fortress in any war is a solid basis for aggressive action, not a place to lock oneself up in, and wait the arrival of the enemy. Once the enemy was there, it would be a different matter. But the enemy wasn't there yet. And, of course, the more aggressively Clive behaved, the greater the number of troops Chunda Sahib would eventually detach from Trichinopoly.

He marched out of the fort with most of his five hundred men and four guns soon after his arrival and found himself face to face with the six hundred horsemen and five hundred infantry of the runaway garrison at Timery, another fort about six miles south-west of Arcot.

The engagement was brief.

His opponents fired off a gun from a great distance, killing a camel, and then vanished into the hot surrounding hills. Clive marched back to his fort.

Clive made a further sortie later on. By now the opposing force had grown to two thousand with two field-guns. There was this time a short sharp battle during which Clive lost some of his small force. Though the enemy retreated once more, he had not sufficient artillery to take Timery itself. He returned once more to Arcot, this time shadowed by opposing cavalry.

The attackers' strength now grew to three thousand, and emboldened by this they moved closer to Arcot, setting up camp within three miles of the fort. They had come, they said, to besiege Clive. But they forgot to post adequate sentries round their camp. At two o'clock in the morning on 12 September, Clive marched out of the fort with the greatest part of his force, and swept down upon the sleeping camp. Surprise was absolute. Chaos followed. The three thousand men fled into the night as fast as they could. By daylight all had gone. Clive did not lose a single man.

In the meantime the Deputy-Governor at Fort St George had sent off the two eighteen-pounder guns. But he could not spare more than a few sepoys to accompany them.

Clive learnt that this small detachment with its two vital guns was held up by a much larger group of Chunda Sahib's men at the Conjeveram pagoda.

He immediately sent thirty European soldiers and fifty sepoys to Conjeveram. The opposing troops retreated to a near-by fort where they were heavily reinforced. It was stalemate. The guns were safe but they could not be moved. They were needed at Arcot.

Clive, with the calculated recklessness that had by now become characteristic, then sent all but eighty men from his garrison to reinforce the party at Conjeveram. They were, whatever happened, to bring those two eighteen-pounders back.

But the opposing commander was beginning to realise

how very much stronger he was than Clive. With some three thousand men at his disposal, and with most of Clive's force struggling to drag the two guns to Arcot, here, surely, was his chance. He hoped, too, that by attacking while most of the garrison was away, the local inhabitants would rise against the defenders.

He threw his whole force, as soon as it was dark, at the fort. Music blared. The hot night air was full of the sound of musketry and the yells of the attackers. It should have been enough to terrify the bravest.

But the defenders remained cool. By lobbing grenades into the advancing cavalry, they panicked the horses and stampeded the following infantry. Though both gates were attacked, neither was breached.

In the morning, the main party from Conjeveram with their two precious eighteen-pounders arrived at the fort. The attackers once more discreetly disappeared. Not a single inhabitant had rebelled.

Chunda Sahib was now really angry. His pride was hurt and he was beginning to lose face. It was intolerable that this part-time Captain-cum-tradesman and a few hundred soldiers of mixed origins should be allowed to sit in his capital, particularly as it had been only recently acquired and at such trouble.

He immediately detached 4,000 of his best cavalry and infantry, added 150 French troops from Pondicherry itself and sent the whole lot off, under the command of his son Rajah Sahib, to Arcot. Here they were joined by the 3,000 men already in the area, and on 23 September 1751, the whole force of over 7,000 men marched into the town, and surrounded the fort, Rajah Sahib himself making his father's palace his headquarters.

Clive's plan was having the desired effect. The pressure was being taken off Trichinopoly. But a problem still remained: if Rajah Sahib captured the fort and returned in triumph to his father, the garrison at Trichinopoly would be worse off than before. It was essential, therefore, to hold the fort at all costs.

Clive, as usual, decided that attack was the best means of defence; and, on 24 September, sallied out of the fort with the greater part of his men, and his four faithful field-guns.

Clive himself led one party straight to the palace gates themselves. Here were posted the French with four field-guns as well. An almost point blank exchange of fire took place. The French retreated into the palace, abandoning the guns. But by now Rajah Sahib, alarmed at the closeness of the fighting to his headquarters, sent in every man he could find. Clive lost fourteen men trying to drag away the abandoned guns. Finally, realising that he could not get them, he returned, under cover of the fire from his own artillery which he had stationed in a three-sided rest-house.

It was on the way back that his life was saved by the devotion of one of his young officers, Lieutenant Trenwith. Trenwith saw one of Rajah Sahib's men taking deliberate aim at Clive from a window of a near-by house. He immediately pulled Clive out of the way, and was himself killed instead.

On entering the fort, Clive was told how another of his young officers, Ensign Glass, with his platoon of thirty men, had successfully routed three to four hundred of the attackers.

The sortie, though hazardous, had succeeded in dislocating Rajah Sahib's plans; but on the next day over 2,000 men from Vellore under Mortazi Ali joined Rajah Sahib. The Indian prince now had 10,000 men at his disposal.

Clive's force in the meantime was down to 320, of which 120 were European and 200 sepoys. Of the eight original officers, only four were now on the active list, Ensign Glass having knocked himself out when a rope broke while he was climbing into the fort, after a vain attempt to blow up some near-by houses used as snipers' nests.

So the siege proper began; 320 men inside, 10,000 outside. Odds thirty to one. And there was enough food in the fort for two months only. If they could last that long. There was plenty of water, but a mason who remained in the fort after the rest of the population had been allowed safe-conduct through the opposing lines, revealed the alarming news that the reservoir could be drained empty, through a pipe running out of the fort. This was hurriedly blocked up.

Rajah Sahib sat down round the fort, waiting for the arrival of his heavy artillery. With this, he felt confident of making a breach and taking the fort by storm. In the meantime, his sharpshooters were instructed to pick off as many of the defenders as possible.

Clive, on his side, issued orders that no man was to show himself unnecessarily; but all the same, sentries had to keep watch. The houses that overlooked the fort were so close that it was enough for a man to show his head to have it blown off. No less than three of Clive's sergeants were killed at different times while accompanying him on his rounds.

Clive himself ignored his own instructions and was frequently seen strolling unconcernedly along the ramparts in full view of snipers, almost, it seemed, daring them to kill him. To the sepoys and to Rajah Sahib's men he seemed immortal, a man who couldn't be killed. Even the more sceptical Europeans thought he bore a charmed life. Perhaps he himself knew that he could not be killed at twenty-five. Perhaps he enjoyed tempting death. Anyhow he had other problems to solve.

The day after Mortazi Ali arrived with his 2,000 men, Clive received a peculiar offer from that dubious man. It was quite simply that Mortazi Ali should come over to Clive's side, if he, Clive, would make a sortie and attack Rajah Sahib. To show the sincerity of his intention Mortazi Ali moved his men to another part of the town.

Clive did not trust Mortazi Ali for one moment, even though it was more than probable that Mortazi Ali and Rajah Sahib hated each other with the usual Indian intensity. However, he saw that this was a good opportunity to put a part of the attackers out of action for a time, and pretended to take the offer seriously. Messages passed to and fro without trouble. Throughout the whole siege, indeed, Clive was able

E

to communicate with whomsoever he pleased, whether it was the opposing commanders, or the Deputy-Governor back in Madras. There was always some way for a man in disguise to slip through the lines at night. In the end, Mortazi Ali realised that Clive was playing the same double-cross game, and returned angrily to his own side. Clive had at least split his opponents and lessened the fire-power against him for a while.

After a fortnight of desultory sniping, the French troops from Pondicherry were reinforced by two eighteen-pounders and seven other heavy calibre guns. On 24 October, these guns began a systematic bombardment against the walls by the north-west gate. The French gunners were so accurate that they knocked out one of Clive's precious eighteen-pounders with their first shot, and disabled the other. After that the guns were pulled out of danger and kept in reserve, thereby leaving the French gunners all the time they needed to batter a breach in the defender's walls. Within six days they had torn a fifty-foot gap in the wall.

But Clive was not to be scared. Taking up a shovel himself and calling upon the few officers still left to him to do the same, he and the rest of the garrison dug trenches and threw up makeshift earthworks, so that when the French artillery had finally demolished the wall Rajah Sahib was faced with a system of trenches that appeared, and probably were, more formidable than the old wall had been. Rajah Sahib decided to wait until a second breach had been made to the south-west before launching an all-out assault.

In the meantime Clive practised what one can only call an act of psychological warfare, and a somewhat comic one at that.

He strengthened with earth the highest towers in the ramparts, and then hauled up on to this mound a vast piece of cannon he had found in the fort. It was reputed to have been presented to Arcot by the Emperor Aurung-Zebe fifty years earlier; and it was said that a thousand oxen had dragged it all the way from Delhi, 1,000 miles.

It fired, if it could fire, huge cannon-balls each weighing seventy-two pounds. Clive loaded the cannon with as much as thirty pounds of powder, rammed in a seventy-two pound cannon-ball, laid a long firing trail and having aimed the heavy thing in the general direction of Rajah Sahib's palace, lit the fuse.

Presently there was a huge explosion, the monstrous cannon-ball sailed through the air, and landed in the middle of the palace while Rajah Sahib was in battle conference with his generals. The conference broke up, and Rajah Sahib, scared stiff, took off to a safer part of the palace.

For the next three days, whenever it was known from observers and spies that Rajah Sahib had convened another conference, the huge gun fired its daily single round. On the fourth day, it blew itself up. It had done its bit.

Outside events were now beginning to take shape. A relief party of 100 Europeans and 200 sepoys was sent out from Madras but was halted by 2,000 of Rajah Sahib's troops.

Of greater significance were the actions of Morari-Roe, the devious but crafty leader of 6,000 Mahrattas, encamped thirty miles from Arcot, waiting to see what happened. He was supposed, officially, to help Mohammed Ali, the English nominee for the Nawabship; but when it seemed as if Mohammed Ali would soon be captured at Trichinoply he had thought it wise to remain neutral.

Clive, however, had a perceptive understanding of strategy. He managed to get a message through to Morari-Roe reminding him of his promise. Morari-Roe, who admired courage and realised that in Clive Mohammed Ali had his best ally, promised to send a detachment of his cavalry to Clive's help.

The threat was enough to send Rajah Sahib into a state of panic. Everyone, Hindu, Mohammedan, prince and peasant, feared these wild and brilliantly led horsemen.

On 30 October, Rajah Sahib sent, under a flag of truce, a message to Clive. It was that Clive should surrender the fort. In return, Rajah Sahib would guarantee Clive and his men a safe-conduct back to Madras; and, as final unanswerable inducement, offered Clive personally a large sum of money.

Clive not only rejected Rajah Sahib's proposals, but added the jibe that he had 'too good an opinion' of Rajah Sahib's character to imagine that he would attempt to storm the fort with 'the rabble' of an army at his disposal.

The rabble in the meantime, under cover of the flag of truce, had come up to the ditch and were trying to persuade Clive's sepoys to desert. Even when the truce party had returned to the palace, some remained by the ditch and were finally dispersed by a volley.

Despite his brave words, Clive was, however, in a precarious position. Sickness and casualties had reduced his small garrison. The walls had been widely breached in two places, the relief party was still held up at Conjeveram and, worst of all, food was running short.

'It is,' said the sepoy's spokesman, 'sufficient for our support, the Europeans require the grain'.

There was nothing now that the troops under Clive's command would not do for him.

Back at Fort St George, however, the East India Company officials were worried and anxious. The Diary and Consultation book for the beginning of November records: '. . . Clive writes from Arcot that he is blockaded and unable to act and therefore we are to be expeditious as possible in relieving him as by delaying, we shall give time to the enemy to gather strength. . . .'

A few days later, the Deputy-Governor ordered Captain Kilpatrick with a further newly-arrived 150 English troops and four field-guns to reinforce the relief party at Conjeveram and march on to Arcot as quickly as possible.

At the same time the Mahrattas, though not exactly coming to Clive's help, indulged in their favourite pastime of plundering and setting houses on fire on the very outskirts of Arcot.

For both Rajah Sahib and Clive the climax was near.

Rajah Sahib decided to make his final assault on the fort

on 14 November. His spies informed him that the garrison was now little more than 200. Despite the detachment sent to Conjeveram to block the relief party, he still had 10,000 men. The odds were now fifty to one. He had, too, his splendid armoured elephants. Nothing would be able to withstand them as they charged the gates. Besides it was a feast day. Anyone who was killed in battle against the unfaithful would by-pass the various purgatories and go straight to heaven. To make matters absolutely sure, plentiful doses of bhang, an earlier form of LSD that stupefied and exhilarated at the same, were issued to the attacking troops. All through the night the noisy preparations for the dawn assault continued.

In the fort all was quiet. But Clive was as busy in other ways. Spies very soon brought him exact information of Rajah Sahib's plans: half the force, led by the elephants, were to attack the two gates. Other forces, were at the same time to assault the two breaches. He had therefore four simultaneous attacks to handle, and he could allocate very few men to any threatened point. He must make up with subtlety what he lacked in numbers.

All through the night, while drums beat outside, and the screams of the drug-impelled attackers increased, Clive and his steady two hundred worked away, quietly and methodically until an hour before dawn when, the last preparations complete, they took a brief rest. Clive went back to his room, and flinging himself fully dressed on his bed, fell asleep immediately.

At dawn the frenzied horde of attackers moved on the fort. Thousands rushed across the dry ditch in front of the first breach. They seemed utterly without sense, many even sitting down in a kind of holy ecstasy on the unprotected fausse-braye between the ditch and the broken ramparts, the rest rushing headlong and screaming into the breach.

Clive's men, crouched in the improvised trenches they had dug beyond, waited until the attackers were almost upon them, and then fired a terrible volley. Muskets, already loaded were handed to the front rank by those standing behind. A second equally terrible volley roared. At the same time two carefully sited guns fired into the attackers.

Men fell dead and wounded. The lines wavered and then came on again and again, only to receive the same relentlessly steady fire. None of the attackers ever reached even the first of the prepared trenches. Fuse-bombs lobbed from the ramparts on to the fausse-braye completed the rout.

At the same time, the two main attacking parties, led by the armoured elephants, rushed at the gates. Again the cool, well-aimed, controlled fire of the defenders was decisive. The mighty elephants, hit in the chinks between the iron plates fixed to their bodies, panicked with pain, and turning, rushed away uncontrollably, trampling all in their path. The terror and confusion caused by these huge bellowing creatures, lurching like stricken monsters amongst their own troops, broke up the attacks on both the gates.

Only at the south-western breach did the attackers appear to be making progress. Here the ditch was full of water and could not be forded. A raft, holding over seventy men was slowly being propelled across the water.

Clive had placed two field-guns in separate towers to cover the ditch; but either through hastiness or nervousness the gunners' aim was bad, and none of the shots hit their target.

Clive, who seemed to be everywhere at the same time, saw that the raft had almost reached the fausse-braye. This was the lightest held of his positions. He had concentrated most of the musketrymen at the gates and the major breach. Seventy determined men landing here could easily overwhelm the dozen or so defenders.

The guns must succeed.

Taking over one of them personally, he aimed with careful coolness at the raft. He fired. The raft rocked as the cannon-ball broke into it. He fired twice again. Each time, he scored a direct hit. The raft disintegrated, flinging its cargo into the moat. Those who were not killed or did not drown, swam back to the further shore.

The attack had lasted an hour.

During it, the garrison fired twelve thousand rounds of musketry, lost four men killed and two wounded.

Rajah Sahib lost four hundred killed and still had not taken the fort.

The French artillerymen took no part in the actual attack. This was partly because their role had been to make the breaches, and partly because, officially, England and France were at peace. In their disguised roles, of 'helping' local princes they did, it is true, come face, from time to time. Only the year before, d'Auteuil, Dupleix's brother-in-law, had found himself opposite a force which he knew included English troops. He had politely sent, under a flag of truce, a request that the English commander should reveal his positions so that 'no European blood should be spilt.' The commander, the now-absent Stringer Lawrence, retorted that if a shot came his way, the French would soon discover where he was.

So at Arcot the French had been breach-makers, not attackers. Now once again, with the assault a failure, the gunners and the musketrymen took over, and kept up during the rest of the day and into the night a desultory fire.

Then suddenly, at two o'clock in the morning, everything became silent.

When dawn came again, Rajah Sahib and his whole army had vanished. His defeat and his fear of the Mahrattas was too much for him. In the hastiness of his retreat, he left behind four pieces of artillery, four mortars and a large quantity of ammunition.

The siege of Arcot was over. It had lasted fifty days.

Chapter 6

Success Follows Success

Kilpatrick arrived the next day with the relief force, but Clive had already gone over to the offensive. He had sent his one remaining subaltern, Bulkley, to Timery. This was the fort that Clive had been unable to capture during his earlier sortie because of the lack of artillery. Now, thanks to the guns Rajah Sahib had left behind, he had plenty. The fort was quickly taken.

Though successful, Clive was aware that the overall strategical position remained fundamentally unchanged. Mohammed Ali was still besieged with Cope and de Gingen in Trichinopoly, Chunda Sahib's army was still intact, de Bussy was still at Hyderabad, Dupleix at Pondicherry.

What had changed, however, were the psychological aspects. Clive's very name was enough to change the allegiance of doubtful States. Morari-Roe made no attempt to conceal his admiration for the Englishman. The powerful Mahratta horsemen were, aι least for the time being, at his disposal.

But there was no time to be lost. Success must be followed by success. Mohammed Ali must be set free, Dupleix thwarted.

Taking command of the reinforcements brought by Kilpatrick, and supported by the Mahratta cavalry, Clive set off by a forced march to intercept a much larger force sent out by Dupleix from Pondicherry to Rajah Sahib's help. It consisted of 2,000 cavalry, 2,500 sepoys and 300 Europeans, mainly French regular troops; nearly 5,000 men in all. Clive's force, even with the Mahratta horsemen, numbered a little over a thousand. But after facing odds of fifty to one, what were five to one?

Clive's unexpected attack had its effect. There was a sharp engagement and the French reinforcements broke and ran. Only darkness saved them from greater destruction as they fled back to Pondicherry pursued by the rapacious Mahrattas. Morari-Roe was more than pleased when he learnt the next day that his detachment with Clive had captured four hundred horses and a hundred thousand rupees from the treasure chests.

For Clive, of greater importance was the promise of the near-by Killahdar or Governor of Arnee to support Mohammed Ali's claim to the throne of the Carnatic. It became even more important now to relieve Trichinopoly. Already the volatile allegiances, until then so strongly French, were turning towards the English. At this battle, French regular troops had been beaten. Dupleix was no longer supreme.

Of more immediate and practical use was the defection of six hundred French-trained sepoys. They came over to the English complete with their arms, and promptly enlisted in Clive's army.

Clive then marched to Conjeveram where a French force still held the famous pagoda. They also held two of Clive's wounded officers, Revel, the artillery officer, and Glass, who had injured himself when the scaling rope broke at Arcot. Both had been captured when being sent back to Fort St David with a number of other wounded. A breach was soon made and the French fled, leaving the two English officers to be rescued and the pagoda to be occupied.

Feeling now that he had done all he could in the Arcot region, Clive marched back to Fort St David to report to the Governor, and to put forward suggestions for the relief of Trichinopoly.

The trouble was that although Mohammed Ali was now promised the support of the powerful Regent of Mysore, neither he nor the English locked up at Trichinopoly made any efforts to get out. They kept quiet even when they knew that Chunda Sahib's besieging army was utterly demoralised by its defeats at Clive's hands. Even too when a strong detachment of Mahratta horsemen managed to join them.

These adventurous semi-robbers, accustomed to Clive's boldness and the material rewards it brought, were disgusted by the supine behaviour of de Gingen and his men. They were not, declared the Mahrattas derisively, 'the same kind of men whom they had seen fight so gallantly at Arcot.'

Clive was eager to mount a strong relief force and to attack the besiegers as soon as possible. Not until Mohammed Ali was relieved and firmly placed on the Carnatic throne instead of Chunda Sahib could the East India Company even begin to feel secure.

Governor Saunders agreed.

But in the meantime Dupleix had not been idle. Chunda Sahib might have failed to take Arcot, the French reinforcements scattered, and Conjeveram captured, but Dupleix was far from beaten. He, like Clive, realised that the solution to the Carnatic problem lay at Trichinopoly. He knew, too, that Clive would soon march to the relief of the fortress. In the present state of low morale, Chunda Sahib's troops would simply run. Something had to be done to divert Clive from his objective and, if possible, revive the morale of Chunda Sahib's army.

Dupleix found the answer in plunder. Providing Chunda Sahib with a strong detachment of French troops and plenty of artillery, he persuaded the Nawab to embark on a campaign of slaughter in the areas that supported Mohammed Ali. Any East India Company properties that were met were also to be destroyed. In this way the English merchants' houses at Poonamalee were burnt to the ground, and the new houses at St Thomé destroyed.

Dupleix's strategem succeeded, at least at first. Clive's force of 80 Europeans, 1,300 sepoys and 6 pieces of field artillery immediately set off in pursuit of the 5,000-strong marauding force. But Rajah Sahib, moving as fast as he could, continually avoided battle and drew Clive away on what appeared to be an aimless chase through the Indian countryside.

Clive moved faster and faster,

Suddenly, at nightfall, near the village of Coverspak, his leading scouts came upon Rajah Sahib's force so unexpectedly that they were momentarily confused by the accurate French artillery fire.

Clive rallied his men and prepared to attack. He saw at once that his small force could not break through with a frontal attack. And, unlike his opponents, he had no cavalry. His only hope lay in getting behind the defenders and attacking from there.

His reconnaissance told him that the flanks were open. Taking six hundred of his best men, he led them, in the moonlight, round to a flank, and set them on their way. In the meantime, he told the rest of his men to keep on firing, so as to give the impression that the main force was still there.

Clive's personal magnetism was so great now that victory was automatically equated with his presence. Conversely, his absence, especially at night, was seen as a sign of defeat. Left alone, the covering party lost heart, and when Clive, satisfied that his flank attack was aimed in the right direction, returned, he found that the covering party had stopped firing and was beginning to give way.

He rallied them quickly, got them to start firing again and kept their opponents busy, until a sudden volley of musketry from behind the French told them that they were surrounded.

Casualties were high on both sides: Clive lost over 70 killed to the 350 of his opponents. But the victory was decisive. Besides taking 60 Frenchmen prisoners and capturing 9 guns Clive showed once and for all that he was able to conduct a full-scale campaign as successfully as he had been able to defend an indefensible fort.

On his way back to Fort St David, the victorious army marched through the town of Dupleix-Fatihabad that the French Governor had erected in his own honour on crowning the Nizam of Hyderabad. The huge monument, commemorating Dupleix's achievements in four languages, was promptly destroyed. With its destruction went also Dupleix's prestige.

Meanwhile, Stringer Lawrence, fit again, landed at Madras on 14 March 1752, a few days after Clive had arrived there to command the Trichinopoly relief force.

Lawrence's arrival with strong reinforcements from England was timely, and Clive immediately placed himself under Lawrence's orders. A curious understanding existed between the two men, despite the differences in character and age. Clive was now twenty-six, Stringer Lawrence fifty-four. Lawrence would unhesitatingly consult Clive on questions of strategy, and Clive would equally unhesitatingly carry out Lawrence's tactical moves.

When some of the more senior regular officers, jealous of Clive's reputation and still looking upon him as a lucky amateur upstart, tried to belittle Clive's defence of Arcot, Stringer Lawrence immediately came to his rescue. He was, declared Lawrence, 'born a soldier, for, without a military education of any sort or much conversing with any of the profession, from his judgement and good sense he led an army like an experienced officer and a brave soldier. . . .'

Clive for his part never forgot Lawrence's defence. Later when, in 1754, the East India Company wanted to present a sword set with diamonds to Clive, he refused to accept it, unless a more magnificent one were presented to Lawrence. Later still when Stringer Lawrence had returned to England and lived not too luxuriously in retirement, Clive made him an annuity of £500 from his private income.

For the present, the urgent business was the relief of Trichinopoly and the defeat of the French. The pretence that the two European powers were merely helping various Indian princes to achieve their ambitions was abandoned. It was, as it had been during the war of the Austrian Succession, French versus English, despite the fact that the two countries were officially at peace.

So, on 17 March 1752, Lawrence and Clive set off with

1,500 men and 8 guns to defeat 21,000 men – of which nearly a thousand were French – and 50 guns. The French were commanded by a man called Jacques Law. He was a brother of that famous Scotsman John Law who, setting himself up as a self-styled financial wizard in Paris, managed with his Mississippi Scheme to ruin so many French investors. This Law, however, was as cautious as the other was daring.

In the ensuing campaign, the two English commanders working in complete harmony, managed, through a series of daring moves, to relieve Trichinopoly and defeat and capture in turn both d'Auteuil and Law.

It was the end for Dupleix's nawab, Chunda Sahib. Abandoned by his earlier supporters, he took refuge with the ruler of Tanjore. The latter immediately tried to sell him to the highest bidder among his enemies. When, however, the Tanjorean found that no one would pay enough for his nawab, he had him beheaded, and sent the decapitated head to Mohammed Ali as a present.

It might now be thought that Mohammed Ali, at last released from Trichinopoly and with his rival dead, could mount the Carnatic throne, but unlike Chunda Sahib who at least was honourable, Mohammed Ali was not. Disputes broke out between him and his new allies, the Mysorians and the Mahrattas.

These were cunningly aggravated by Dupleix, and particularly by his clever wife, so that fighting still went on. It was not until Clive had captured the two great fortresses of Covelong and Chingliput, with recruits from England so raw that at first they ran away at the sound of their own guns, that Mohammed Ali finally became Nawab of the Carnatic.

But even then Dupleix did not give up. He may have lost control of the Carnatic, but de Bussy was still at Hyderabad, and as long as intrigue were possible, he swore he would go on intriguing against the East India Company, and one day restore the French position in the Carnatic.

Chapter 7

'General' Clive

Clive was now a famous young man. The news of his astonishing defence of Arcot and subsequent victories had spread from the Coromandel Coast to other parts of India. French military superiority had been taken for granted so long that it came as a considerable shock to realise that they had been halted and defeated by an 'amateur' soldier with very few trained troops at his disposal.

His fame reached England. His defence of Arcot was just the kind of exploit to cheer the public at home. Here was an exciting new figure, a dashing young man gaining victories in a strange country. The memory of the Duke of Cumberland's defeat by the French at Fontenoy, seven years earlier in the terrible year of the Jacobite Rebellion when the Scots army reached Rugby, still rankled. The fact that England and France were officially at peace, added to the piquancy of the situation. He became immediately a popular hero-figure.

His father wrote excitedly to him on 15 December 1752: '. . . you are compared to no less than some of those brave generals who are gone, but left their names upon record to their glory and honour.'

At the same time, in case his son was thinking of coming home, he added: '. . . your friends, among which is one of the principal directors, and my intimate acquaintance, advise you that you should not leave Madras before you know how the directors propose to reward you. . . .'

All the father's antipathy for his eldest son was melting in the warm sunshine of Clive's popularity.

His mother wrote, on the next day, with more feeling and honesty: '. . . your brave conduct, and success which Providence has blessed you with, is the talk and wonder of the public, the great joy and satisfaction of your friends: but more particularly so to me, as it gives me hope of seeing you much sooner than I could possibly have expected.'

But while all this excitement was going on elsewhere, Clive himself was suffering from battle-fatigue. He had been in almost continuous action for over a year. He was a captive of his own reputation. His daring, his bravery, his contempt for his opponents were now taken for granted. He was expected to take risks, to perform acts of courage that would have seemed sublime in other men.

The training of those awful recruits, press-ganged from the streets of London or recently released from prison, had been the worst test of all. To stop them running, or hiding in wells as one of them did for twenty-four hours, he had to take extra risks, to show by his own indifference to danger that they had nothing to fear. No other officer would, or could, have taken on such an appalling task. But he had succeeded in turning them into soldiers, and they had in the end taken the last two great forts left to the French. But now, by the autumn of 1752, he was tired out. His old sickness had returned.

His ambitions had never been purely military. He had none of the regular army officer's outlook on promotion. He had come to India to make his fortune. Now, after eight years in this hot and clammy climate, he was at last in a position to do so.

He had kept his position as a covenanted servant of the East India Company. Now he had been promoted to Junior Merchant. His salary was £30 a year. More significantly, he was allowed to trade on his own account.

He had gone into partnership with Robert Orme. Orme was young like himself, and keen to make a fortune. He was later on to write a full and very detailed account of Clive's campaigns. But at the moment his concern was to make the firm of Robert Orme and Clive successful. They ran an import-export business in all kinds of goods between the

1a   The headquarters of the East India Company, as it was when Clive joined the service. Larger premises were subsequently built. The East India Company remained in existence until the middle of the nineteenth century. *(India Records Office)*

1b   An 'East Indiaman' similar to the ship in which Clive first sailed for India. These ships were entirely financed and maintained by the East India Company. Many of them were heavily armed. *(National Maritime Museum)*

2a Dupleix, the French
Governor of Pondicherry
and Clive's great rival for
some years. He was handi-
capped by the indifference
of his home Government.
(India Records Office)

2b Admiral Boscawen, in command of the
British naval forces off Madras in 1749.
He was later to win a great naval victory
against the French fleet in European
waters, off Quiberon Bay on 22nd November, 1759. *(National Portrait Gallery)*

3a Colonel Stringer Lawrence, Clive's first military Commander, who later became one of his firm friends. Colonel Lawrence has always been considered to be the father of the British Army in India. *(National Portrait Gallery)*

3b Portrait of Clive about the age of forty. Many engravings were made after his triumphant return to England in 1760, and granting of a title. *(India Records Office)*

4   Palladian Gardens near Madras—typical of the houses owned by the rich merchants of eighteenth-century India. Many of the houses were copies of European buildings, and constructed by local builders who had never seen, let alone built, a European house. *(India Records Office)*

Coromandel Coast and Bengal, eight hundred miles to the north. Orme operated from peaceful Calcutta, Clive, when his military duties permitted, from turbulent Madras. Even at the height of the fighting the firm was making money. By the middle of 1752 Clive had a personal fortune, from trade and prize-money, of £40,000 (£400,000 today). He now owned one of the best houses in Madras.

Finally, he was in love.

One day, earlier that year, he had found Edmund Maskelyne looking at a miniature of a beautiful young girl.

'Who is she?' asked Clive.

'My sister', said Maskelyne.

Clive stared at the miniature for a long time.

'Invite her here', he said. 'I would like to marry her.'

Half-jokingly, half-seriously Edmund Maskelyne did that; and in June 1752, the beautiful Margaret Maskelyne from Purton in Wiltshire arrived. With her arrived ten other eligible young ladies, 'the Fishing Fleet' looking for husbands.

Dalton, another young officer and friend of Clive's, locked up at the time with Mohammed Ali and de Gingen in Trichinopoly, wrote to Clive: 'By this time I reckon you are able to give one an account of the new arrived angels – by God, it would be a good joke if your countenance was to smite one of them, and you were to commit matrimony. . . .'

He had addressed Clive ironically as 'Dear Beauty'.

His countenance did indeed 'smite' Margaret Maskelyne, or more correctly his character and person. She was eager to meet her brother's famous friend, the man the whole of England was talking about. She came from an old family that had held their Wiltshire estate for many generations. As was usual, it descended from eldest son to eldest son. This meant that the other members had to find occupations elsewhere. Some went into the Law; others into Government and other service. Her own father worked for many years in the Secretary of State's office in Whitehall.

The Maskelyne connection with the East India Company

F

was already well established. One of her uncles had died at the now abandoned factory of Fort Marlborough on the north coast of Sumatra in 1729. Two of her aunts had married in India, one, Elizabeth, at this very same Fort St George. There was therefore nothing unusual in her visiting Madras, amongst other places, in the usual young lady's occupation of those days of finding a husband.

He, on his side, was equally 'smitten'. She was exceedingly beautiful, even more beautiful than in her miniature. She was kind, considerate, witty and talented. In addition, though this was not to be known till later, she had a steadfastness that was to help him through many painful experiences.

He courted her with the same dashing ardour he brought into all his activities, returning to her whenever he could. He proposed and was accepted.

But he was still desperately ill from strain and overwork. He was taking more and more opium to kill the pain in his stomach. Now it would need more than a cruise in the Bay of Bengal to cure. After eight years continuous service in India, it was time he went back to England.

Margaret, too, advised a return. She could see that another year in Madras might easily kill him. He would become then just another European victim of the Coromandel Coast.

He had already applied for release from military duties. The Fort St David diary records for 9 October 1752: 'Captain Clive complain'd (by letter) of Wont of Health and desired to return: which as he had executed his Plan, was granted.'

Later he made a formal application to be allowed to return to England and this too was granted.

He and Margaret were married in the little church at Fort St George on 18 February 1753. The Governor, Maskelyne, Dalton and his other friends and admirers, for he was no longer short of either, added their wishes for a long, happy and prosperous marriage.

Stringer Lawrence summed up what everyone felt, when

he wrote saying, in his blunt, unimaginative way, that he 'sincerely rejoiced that both had met with such good fortune.'

They spent their last few weeks in India at Madras on an unofficial honeymoon, while waiting to board ship for England.

Then, on 23 March 1753, Robert and Margaret Clive sailed from Madras on board the *Bombay Castle* for Cape Town. They reached Cape Town two and a half months later. Here they changed to the more comfortable *Pelham* on 10 June, and after a pleasant journey landed at Erith on 14 October, nearly seven months after leaving Madras.

It was just over ten years since he had sailed poor, unknown, lonely and homesick, for India. Now he was returning rich, famous, married and eager for life. Everything was now possible.

They called first on his parents. His father, impractical as ever, had taken a large house in Swithen's Lane, London, near, as his mother had written in her letter, 'the post house'. Here lived four of Clive's sisters as well as his father and mother. The house was big, unwieldy, far away from the smart part of the town.

Clive's fortune of £40,000 had come back mainly in diamonds, a favourite means of transporting money in those risky days. He had left enough cash in India for further investments in diamonds to be made.

He now came to the rescue of his financially unstable father. He paid off the mortgages on the Styche estate, and various other debts, and thus made it possible for Richard Clive to live like the country gentleman he wished to be.

Richard Clive's earlier contempt for his eldest son now turned to excessive pride. He never ceased to speak, probably much to the boredom of his listeners, about Robert's success both as a commander and as a businessman. But he was as puzzled as ever. How could the Booby, with no education, have done so well, while he, Richard, who had trained at the Bar, had in the end to be rescued and pensioned off by his own son?

His mother had never ceased, in the past, to defend and protect him. His present success was a vindication of all her previous beliefs. Her husband's new-found pride in his eldest son amused her. It also made life much easier.

Robert Clive now bought for himself a house in fashionable Queen Square, near St James's Park, and he and his young bride threw themselves eagerly into society life.

It was the time when the great Dr Johnson dominated intellectual life. Great painters like Reynolds and Gainsborough were there to portray the famous and rich. 'Beau' Nash was the leader of taste, the 'trend-setter' of the day was David Garrick the leading actor-manager. Hogarth satirised the less glamorous side of life.

Robert Clive and his wife lived in great style in their fine house near St James's Park. They entertained magnificently and lavishly even in those wealthy days. Despite his somewhat unprepossessing appearance, Clive spent vast sums on wigs and clothes. Though 'Beau' Nash might consider him ostentatious, Clive did not care. He was enjoying himself. His horses were among the finest in London, and he and Margaret would drive through the admiring crowds enjoying their popularity.

Nor were the East India Company directors slow in showing their appreciation to the man who had saved them on the Coromandel Coast. They gave a great dinner in his honour in the City. At the end of it they toasted him, as his father had told him was their practice, as 'General Clive'. In February 1754 the Court of Directors voted him that famous sword set with diamonds 'as a token of their esteem, and of their sense of his singular services to the Company on the coast of the Coromandel'. This was the one he would not accept unless Stringer Lawrence were presented with an even better one. Somewhat relectantly, no doubt, the thrifty directors had to vote a further large sum for a second sword.

More appositely perhaps, they told Clive that they would welcome him back, whenever he liked. But he had other plans.

France and England were officially at peace. Only in the Carnatic had the war gone on unofficially between the two countries; and this had been mainly due to Dupleix's disregard of his own Government's instructions.

For some time Lord Holderness, the assistant to the Secretary of War, had been negotiating with the French Government to bring this private war to an end. Holderness called upon Clive to gain first-hand information about conditions in the Carnatic.

Through Holderness, Clive met Henry Fox, the Secretary for War, himself.

The political situation at the time was somewhat peculiar. The Whigs were in almost complete control. The Jacobites had been discredited by the '45 Rebellion, and the Tory Party hardly existed. But this outward unity merely hid inner rivalries and hatreds. The Prime Minister, the Duke of Newcastle, was weak, indecisive, vacillating, but stubborn. Henry Fox was tough, able and ambitious. Though a member of Newcastle's Cabinet, he never ceased to intrigue against his nominal leader.

Fox suggested that Clive should stand for Parliament, and Clive agreed.

It was just a question of finding a suitable rotten borough that could offer him a seat. Fox's friend, Lord Sandwich, had large estates in the West Country. A borough was soon found in Cornwall.

There were four candidates. All were Whigs. Two of them, Clive and Stevenson, were Fox's nominees. Two others, Luttrell and Hussey, the nominees of the Duke of Newcastle.

The usual bribery and corruption occurred, Clive having to lay out large sums of money in support of his candidature. But it would, he was told, be worth it; for politics was merely the first step to a position of wealth and power. Once a man of his reputation was in Parliament, nothing would be impossible.

Clive's head was already turned. Though both his wife and mother tried to warn him of the dangers of flattery and success, he would not listen to them. His self-confidence was unshakable. He would succeed in England, just as he had succeeded in India.

When the election results came in, he and Stevenson had received thirty votes. This was more than enough for success. Their opponents had only collected twenty-five.

He was in.

There were complaints that the voting had been rigged, which of course it had been, by all concerned. A committee of investigation was formed. Fox was a member of this committee. It soon became obvious that the real protagonists were Fox and Newcastle, the goal, control of the House of Commons.

Fox's eloquence carried the committee, but when the committee's findings came to the vote in the House of Commons, the few Tories still there voted for Newcastle, They disliked all Whigs, but their dislike for Sandwich and Fox was greater than their dislike for Newcastle.

Clive lost his seat.

This was a severe set-back. The £40,000 he had brought back to England had largely vanished. His generosity, his extravagant way of life and now the huge bribes he had had to disburse in the recent Hogarthian-type election, had left him very short of cash.

There was only one thing for it: he must start all over again.

He was anyhow tired of the smart London life. Never good in society, he was now disillusioned by its falseness. There was renewed talk of war between England and France. As long as there was one Frenchman in India, the East India Company's position would always be threatened.

He went to the Company and offered his services. They were gratefully received. He was appointed Governor of Fort St David, and, in order to make his relationship with future 'professional' army officers secure, was granted a commission as a Lieutenant-Colonel of Foot.

On 5 April 1755, he and Margaret boarded the *Stretham,* and sailed eighteen days later. They were given a nine-gun salute. Their farewell to England was made unhappy for them, because they had to leave behind their two young sons. The doctors decreed that they were not strong enough to face the Indian climate. Edward, the first born, was a year old; the younger boy only a few weeks old. He was to die before they reached India.

Part Two

The Victor of Plassey

Chapter 8

Malabar then St David

There was one significant change in India since Clive had last been there: Dupleix had gone.

He had been recalled to France in 1754, his Government finally deciding that he could not be allowed to carry on his private war against the English. Holderness, from London, had pointed out the anomaly of being everywhere at peace with France, except in India. Dupleix himself, in repeated despatches, had assured the Ministers in Paris that the East India Company was at its last gasp.

In fact, the opposite had happened. Stringer Lawrence, Kilpatrick, Caillaud and Dalton had been fighting all through 1753 and 1754 with increasing success. Far from the English being at their last gasp, it was the French who were in despair.

Dupleix had had the vision to see ahead of events. At the same time he had the energy and guile to put this vision into effect. By 1752, he had acquired for France an area of land as big as the mother country herself. But this he saw only as the beginning. He dreamed of France controlling, through him, the whole Mogul Empire.

Alas, for Dupleix, his king was Louis XV, sometimes called the worst king who ever reigned. It was not perhaps his fault. He had become King at the age of five, on the death of his great-grandfather Louis XIV, 'Le Roi Soleil', the monarch who said, simply 'l'Etat, c'est moi', the man who had built Versailles and raised the name of the French monarchy above that of any other.

How could a five-year-old boy, delicate and unsure of himself, hope to compare to so famous a man? For the first few years of his reign, a Regency acted on his behalf, but in 1723, at the age of thirteen, he became absolute. His old tutor, Cardinal Fleury, in fact ruled in his name, and when he died at over ninety in 1743, it was Madame de Pompadour, Louis XV's official mistress, who became the real power in France.

Her suite was immediately above the King's in that large, but extraordinarily uncomfortable and insanitary Palace of Versailles. As soon as the courtiers had attended the King's rising, they would rush upstairs to present their compliments to Madame de Pompadour. It was she who made and unmade ministers. She was not, in herself, a bad woman; but she lacked knowledge, particularly of foreign affairs. Her main efforts were concerned with keeping the King quiet, and herself in power. She managed both until her death in 1764.

Dupleix returned to France, discredited and unpopular. He was not, like La Bourdonnais, thrown into the Bastille; but, immediately on his return, pushed to one side and ignored. While his great rival Clive was fêted by London, Dupleix was hated by Paris.

He lived on, in considerable financial difficulties, until 1763. A few days before he died, he wrote: 'I have given my youth, my fortune, my life to enrich my country in Asia. My services are treated as fables, and I as the vilest of mankind.'

He deserved a better fate.

In the meantime, another Governor had been sent out to Pondicherry: Monsieur Godeheu.

In a letter to George Pigot, at Vizagapatam, the Governor of Fort St George wrote, on 22 August 1754: 'Mr Dupleix is dismissed from his Government and is succeeded in it by Mons Godeheu lately arrived from France, he speaks in a very pacifick Stile and we shall not be backward in Answering his Intensions if they really tend to the restoring tranquility on just and honourable terms but we shall be on our guard & place no more confidence on Gallic Declarations than they deserve.'

Godeheu was as 'pacifick' as he promised, and did

everything to undo Dupleix's achievements in India. In December 1754 he and Thomas Saunders, now the Governor of Fort St George, signed a private treaty agreeing that neither the English nor the French should interfere any more in the squabbles between Indian States. For the first time for many years each company was able to trade, once again, in peace.

Although appointed Governor of Fort St David, Clive landed on 27 November 1755 at Bombay, on the west coast of India, six hundred miles across country from Madras. He had with him three companies of Royal Artillery and three hundred infantry.

There was a reason for this.

Although Dupleix had gone, the crafty de Bussy was still an 'advisor' at Hyderabad. This meant, in effect, that de Bussy controlled that huge central State and could threaten the west, south and east coasts of India whenever he wished. In the expected event of a renewal of war between France and England this fact might be decisive.

The East India Company proposed therefore to 'remove' de Bussy by the usual stratagem of supposedly supporting the rivals to the Nizam of Hyderabad. The Government agreed, but argued that a certain Colonel Scott, who had sailed for India the year before, should be in charge of the expedition. Scott was senior to Clive. He also had a strong ally in the person of the Duke of Cumberland. Though able, he was an engineer, and unfortunately had no command experience.

However, the Directors sent Clive to Bombay all the same, hoping that something might happen to change the situation.

Something did happen: Scott died before Clive reached India. The question of command was thus resolved, there being no other claimants to the position.

But the plan, all the same, had to be abandoned because the Bombay authorities refused to sanction any action that might disrupt the Saunders-Godeheu treaty.

What, Clive wondered, could he do instead?

South of Bombay runs the Malabar Coast, a wild rocky shore that for many years had been the refuge of pirates. They would emerge from their well-sited fortresses, attack ships trading along the coast and return to their strongholds before they could be intercepted.

For years the English, Dutch and Portuguese fleets had tried unsuccessfully to capture these fortified harbours. The pirates were controlled by the Angria family, a courageous and crafty lot of mixed Mahratta, Arab and Portuguese blood. They had taken the precaution of recognising the authority of the Peshwas, who controlled the land behind them. This meant that their forts could not be attacked from the land-side and they were impregnable from the sea.

They could therefore sail in their swift ships to any part of the Malabar Coast, land unexpectedly at an undefended town, burn and plunder it, and get away with their loot, before the alarm was given.

This had been going on for forty years, and the Angria family had grown wealthy and arrogant, sure of their power, confident that they could plunder towns and prey on shipping for ever.

But in 1750, Tulaji Angria, the latest leader of this predatory family, quarrelled with the Peshwas, and refused any longer to accept their authority.

This was the chance for which the Europeans had been waiting. An English fleet under the command of Commodore James and supported by the Mahrattas, captured the island fortress of Suvarnadrug, eighty miles south of Bombay, a few months before Clive arrived in Bombay.

With his arrival, a more ambitious plan was suggested. Tulaji Angria had retreated to Gheria, a fort lower down the coast. It was built on a huge rock and was considered inaccessible from the sea. The plan was to capture Gheria.

The overall commander at Bombay was Admiral Watson. He and Clive now met for the first time. They were to meet and work together many times in the future.

Watson was about forty-four at the time. He was a large

plump moon-faced man, with an extraordinary small, almost pouting mouth. His father was Dr John Watson, Prebendary of Westminster. An uncle was First Lord of the Admiralty. His rise to the rank of Admiral had been commendably rapid. He had the professional military man's arrogance, particularly where other officers were concerned. He was utterly convinced, and did not hesitate to say so, that a regular officer was far superior to any other kind of officer. He had little or no time for subtleties. Gruff, outspoken, easily offended, he liked to get on with the job. Yet he could show, as if his early religious training still counted, moments of kindness, even of sentimentality. It was said that he tried to prevent a widow from allowing herself to be killed when her husband died, and that he distributed his own medicines in case of need.

But he could be obstinate and obstructive.

Of a meticulous turn of mind, he liked to get all the details of a campaign carefully worked out in advance, especially those concerning prize-money and plunder; for like every naval and army commander operating in the East, plunder was the main concern. It might be beneficial to clear the Malabar Coast of Angria's pirates, but it would have to be profitable if it were to be done.

More important still, in Watson's eyes the exact proportion to be paid to each participant had to be worked out, As an Admiral, he would get the biggest share, Vice-Admiral Pocock, his second-in-command, would get the next biggest share. Clive, as a Lieutenant-Colonel in the Army ranked only, in the Navy's eyes, as a Naval Captain with under three years' service. His share would thus be much less.

Trouble broke out immediately. Clive claimed that, as the senior Army commander, he should have at least the same amount as Pocock. He was not motivated entirely by the need for more cash, although after his London extravagance he could well do with it. It was, he declared, a question of the Army's honour.

Watson retorted that his actions were dictated solely for

the honour of the Navy. What on earth would happen if mere Lieutenant-Colonels were allowed as much plunder as Vice-Admirals? The whole system of rewards would collapse.

The somewhat ludicrous quarrel spread to the more junior ranks of both the Navy and the Army. At one time, so bitter became the recriminations that it seemed as if the expedition would never get started at all.

Admiral Watson would not give an inch. Nor would Clive. Honour seemed about to wreck what expediency proposed.

Then Watson offered to pay the difference between Clive and Pocock's share, from his own pocket. In this way, the principle of the Navy's superior claims would be established, while Clive would not suffer personally.

Clive, eager to get on with the campaign and not wishing to disrupt relations between the Army and the Navy any further, accepted the compromise in principle, but said that he would not take any of Watson's cash.

The first of many rows between these two somewhat irascible commanders was over. The expedition could get under way at last.

On 7 February 1756, Admiral Watson sailed from Bombay with fourteen ships. Four of them had fifty or more guns each. On board were 800 European and 1,000 Indian troops, under Clive's command.

Gheria seemed completely impregnable as it loomed up from the sea. But now that the Peshwas no longer guaranteed the safety of the land approach, it was not as formidable as it looked.

On 12 February, Watson opened a bombardment. Clive landed with his troops. Within two days the 'impregnable' fortress had fallen, and Angria had fled. Watson sailed on down the Malabar Coast, capturing the rest of Angria's forts, and destroying his fleets. The pirate menace was at an end. The plunder and prize-money was duly shared out among the victors, Clive steadfastly refusing to take a penny of Watson's personal money.

5   Tanjore soldier depicted here with his wife. Each Indian ruler raised and paid for his own army. Uniforms were a question of the ruler's personal choice. *(India Records Office)*

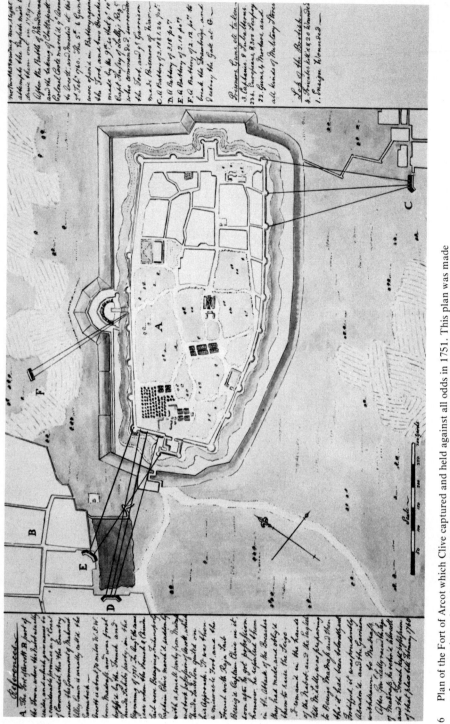

6   Plan of the Fort of Arcot which Clive captured and held against all odds in 1751. This plan was made a few years later, but the details had not changed since the time Clive was there. *(India Records Office)*

7 View of Fort Trichinopoly. It was in order to relieve pressure on the besieged British troops in the fort that Clive made his famous dash for Arcot. *(National Army Museum)*

8   'The Good Life'—High Society in Regent's Park. The luxurious extravagance of life at the time
produced a whole breed of sharp pencilled caricaturists. *(Radio Times Hulton Picture Library)*

There was nothing more for Clive to do on the Malabar Coast. It was time anyhow to take up his appointment as Governor of Fort St David.

He and Margaret sailed via Cape Cormorin for Fort St George. Here they landed and renewed old friendships. Clive attended a number of consultations, or board meetings, of the Council of Fort St George. George Pigot, who had accompanied him on the dangerous reconnaissance to Trichinopoly, was now Governor. Stringer Lawrence, whose health was giving cause for concern, was also a member. So was Robert Orme.

Then once again he and Margaret sailed south, this time for Fort St David, where he arrived on 22 June and, according to the Diary of Consultation book of Fort St George, was 'received with the usual Honours'.

Now started a few months of calm for Clive and his wife. Perhaps, seen in retrospect, it was the traditional ominous calm before the storm. The first monsoon had started. Though hot as always, the little seaside fort was habitable. After the two years' absence, Clive's health was now first-class again. He was not taking drugs any more. He was happily married. If his wife missed the baby still alive in England, she never showed it to her husband. This was the place her brother and husband had reached on the fall of Madras nearly ten years earlier. He had then been a clerk. Now he was the Governor. That was enough.

His main concern was drawing up a list of the Company's plate silver, cutlery and furniture at Fort St David, and suggesting that a new lot should be sent.

But in the background there was always the threat of renewed war with France.

Yet, the crisis came, eventually, from a different and completely unexpected quarter.

First news of it was received by the Council of Fort St George in a letter from William Watts dated 2 July 1756, and received, because of the slow means of travel, on 17 August 1756. It began: 'It is with the utmost concern we now inform you that Fort William was taken by the Moors the 20th Ultimo.'

There was immediate consternation and disbelief. Eyes turned to the map of the mouth of the Ganges, eight hundred miles to the north.

Unlike the factories on the Coromandel Coast, there had never been any trouble at Fort William or Calcutta. Even the French at near-by Chandernagore had not given any trouble. Both the Dutch at Chinsura and the Danes at Serampore, had been model neighbours.

Relations with the Company's landlord, the Nawabs of Bengal, had always been good. Even the wild plundering Mahrattas had not been able to reach Calcutta. The great fertile hinterland along the Ganges, the richest part of India, had been a source of mutual trade and profit for over fifty years.

And then suddenly this.

What had happened?

Aliverdi Khan, who had ruled Bengal and Orissa for fifteen years, died on 9 April 1756. He was immediately succeeded by his grandson Siraj-ud-dowla. As so often with Mohammedan princes, he had a number of other names, including Mirza Mahmud, but he is best known as Siraj-ud-dowla, which means 'the sun of the State.' To the English soldiers and sailors who were to get to know him, he was known by the more pronounceable name of 'Sir Roger Dowler'.

Siraj-ud-dowla was just over twenty-one when he succeeded his grandfather. He had no real claim to the Nawabship, as he was illegitimate. He had no following, but was merely put there by the ruling Mohammedan clique. The power of the Moguls in Delhi had declined to such an extent that he felt insecure in the predominantly Hindu State of Bengal.

He had not the intellectual power to understand that the situation had changed since his grandfather came to the throne. The most powerful men in Bengal were now a class of bania, or professional traders, who were in close touch with the European factories.

They handled all the trade conducted by the foreign companies. They were neither Mohammedans nor Bengalis; but were Marwaris who came from Rajputana, on the other side of India, a thousand miles away.

Siraj-ud-dowla suspected, not without reason, that these Marwari merchants would like to see him overthrown. They were not the only ones. But they were the most powerful; and the Nawab had foolishly insulted one of them, the legendary Jagat Seth, founder of the millionaire family of that name.

Another Marwari also makes his appearance at this time: Omi Chand. He was a go-between, acting both for the Nawab and the European companies, a man judged unreliable even where deviousness was considered normal. He was to play an increasingly significant role in Bengali affairs in the near future.

At the time, however, he was content to collect from both sides, to be a conveyor of news and gossip, to intrigue and to amass a fortune.

It was undoubtedly he who told Siraj-ud-dowla of the enormous profits of the European companies, particularly the East India Company, and perhaps first put the idea of moving against the Company into the Nawab's head.

At all events, Siraj-ud-dowla did not hesitate. He quickly found a pretext for taking action. For some time both the French and the English companies, in anticipation of the coming war, had been strengthening their forts.

Siraj-ud-dowla ordered them to stop doing so at once.

The French complied. Chandernagore was anyhow in a good state of repair, and the work was carried on surreptitiously as soon as the Nawab's delegation had gone.

The English, on the other hand, pointed out that by the decree of 1696 they were allowed to fortify Calcutta, that the fort was in a bad state of repair, and that they were merely bringing it up to date.

This 'defiance' on the part of his tenant was enough for

93

Siraj-ud-dowla. He immediately surrounded Cossimbazar with, as William Watts puts it, '10,000 Horse and 20,000 Rageput Gun Men', ordered Watts and his assistant Collet to report to him, and had them both imprisoned.

He then marched on Calcutta.

Panic immediately took possession of the whole European and Marwari community. There was only one thought in everybody's mind: get as far away, as quickly as possible from the advancing Nawab. There was a rush for the ships on the Hooghli. Everyone, including the Governor of Fort William, Drake, and the military commander, Captain Minchin, fought for a place on the ships.

The panic spread to the ship's captains. They began sailing downstream leaving behind at Fort William over 150 men, and one woman who refused to leave her husband.

The Nawab's army took Calcutta almost without a fight and moved on to Fort William some miles downstream. At no time, during the next two days, when the fort surrendered, was any effort made by the ships to return to rescue those who had been left behind.

It remained for an ex-surgeon called Holwell, a member of the Council of the East India Company, to take charge of the defence of Fort William.

But he had neither the military knowledge nor leadership to inspire confidence in the few who had remained. He could not control those under his command. Some took to drink. Some to plunder. Some despaired. There was no Clive there – he was in fact at that very moment approaching Fort St David to take up his Governorship – to inspire them, and make the impossible possible.

Holwell tried to negotiate an orderly surrender of the fort, but before he could receive an answer from Siraj-ud-dowla, the Nawab's army stormed and captured the fort.

What happened next has been subject of dispute and contention ever since.

According to Holwell himself, he was taken – his hands bound – to the Nawab. The latter immediately had Holwell's hands untied, and told him that he and his companions had nothing to fear.

They were then led away.

Nearby was a small prison with a room measuring twenty feet by twenty feet. It had two small windows. It was used by the English to lock up, from time to time, the odd felon caught stealing Company property.

It was known locally as the Black Hole.

Some search was made for suitable accommodation where the prisoners could be kept for the night, but none could be found. There was only this small prison room.

The men in charge of the prisoners had been told to lock them up for the night. Lock them up they would. The fact that the room could hold ten, twenty at the most, did not matter. Orders were orders.

The 146 prisoners were crammed into the room. The doors were locked. They were left there for the night.

One of the survivors later reported to Parliament what happened, in the following laconic fashion: 'Some of our company expired very soon after being put in: others grew mad, and having lost their senses, died in high delirium. All we could urge to the guard set over us, could not prevail upon them either to set us at liberty, or separate us into different prisons; which we desired, and offered money to obtain; but to no purpose: and when we were released at eight o'clock the next morning, only twenty-three came out alive.'

The account, unemotional and factual, can give no idea of the horror of that hot still night when that claustrophobic body of prisoners fought for air, water and life, while the uncomprehending guards stood helplessly by 'carrying out orders'.

Some historians have since tried to minimise the tragedy. Some have maintained that it never occurred at all, that it was merely a bit of 'war propaganda' dreamt up by Holwell himself. Others have claimed that the numbers were less than quoted. A figure of seventy is mentioned.

There is no doubt that Siraj-ud-dowla himself was unaware of what was happening. He had treated Holwell with the normal courtesies accorded to the vanquished, and had merely instructed that the prisoners should be locked up for the night.

It was some probably not very intelligent subordinate who, finding nothing more suitable, had obeyed the order in too literal a fashion. Later, no one had dared to take the responsibility of releasing the prisoners on their own initiative. Tragedies are often caused by such acts of bureaucratic inefficiency.

Whatever the number thrust into that tiny room, all accounts are agreed that only twenty-three came out alive. It was this that mattered.

Siraj-ud-dowla's troops undoubtedly committed many acts of cruelty when they over-ran Cossimbazar, Calcutta and Fort William. Siraj-ud-dowla himself was arrogant, greedy and headstrong. Mir Jaffar, his Commander-in-Chief, was ruthless. The English Governor, Roger Drake, his military commander and the ships' captains, were guilty of varying degrees of cowardice. The population panicked. No one came out of it well.

But when all the horror stories were told, the last rumours proved or disproved, it was this one shattering night of horrific imprisonment that remained in the minds of men at the time, and has since gone down in history as the Black Hole of Calcutta.

Chapter 9

The Relief of Calcutta

As soon as George Pigot, Stringer Lawrence and the other members of the Council at Madras had read William Watt's letter, they decided that an expedition must be sent as soon as possible to Calcutta to regain the lost factory and avenge the deaths of their countrymen.

Many of those who had died had been members of the East India Company. All were acquaintances. Some were friends. The flight of the Governor and the fact that most could have been saved had the ships come back for them added to the bitterness of the Council. For years now, the East India Company merchants who served on the Coromandel Coast had faced enemies of every kind from the French to the Mahrattas and the Poligars. Calcutta and Bengal had seemed like a peaceful Paradise. Yet when the first threat came, it had panicked.

The Council thought that one fifty-gun ship would be sufficient to scare away any of Siraj-ud-dowla's men holding Fort William, and accordingly sent a note to Admiral of the Red, Charles Watson, anchored off Madras with his squadron.

Watson replied that he was always 'ready and willing at all times to do everything in his Power for the Service of the Company but considering the State of Affairs in Europe it appear'd quite necessary his Squadron should not be divided. . . .'

The Council had come up against the first obstacle. It was one thing to decide on an expedition; it was quite another to get it started.

Watson however had a point. War with France was

almost upon them. It would have been folly to split his command.

The Council then asked him whether he would be prepared to sail with his whole squadron.

Watson agreed.

They had surmounted the first obstacle.

There was a much more difficult one ahead: the choice of military commander.

Stringer Lawrence, the obvious first choice, was far from well. Besides he would be needed at Madras should the war with France really come. The Council decided unanimously to call upon Clive, and summoned him urgently from Fort St David.

And that was where the trouble started, for also at Madras was Colonel John Aldercron, the commanding officer of the 39th Foot.

The 39th Foot – now part of the Devonshire and Dorset Regiment – was the first regular battalion to be sent to India. Aldercron, from all accounts, was not only incompetent but extremely obstructive. Although he had no experience of Indian field conditions, he insisted that he should be in command of any military operations that were being planned. He was after all, as he pointed out incessantly, the senior military commander; indeed, he was the only senior regular officer it was true but had resigned and taken up a quasi-officer it was true but has resigned and taken up a quasi-military post with the East India Company.

Aldercron, like all regular officers, had a deep contempt for merchants ('Box-wallahs' as they were to be called at a later date) especially when they dressed up as soldiers. Matters had not been helped when Stringer Lawrence had refused to serve under Aldercron, and contented himself with commanding the East India Company forces. As for Clive, argued Aldercron, why he wasn't even a soldier at all. He may have had a few lucky successes with small numbers of troops in obscure jungle skirmishes, but what did he know of military lore? His promotion to Lieutenant-Colonel was merely a paper transaction. He couldn't possible be taken seriously as a commander-in-chief of an army that included regular troops of the King.

Pigot and his colleagues were equally distrustful of Aldercron. They were quite determined that they would not have him as their commander. But they did want the 39th Foot and the considerable artillery that went with the regiment. Only the most careful and tactful negotiations could have solved the impasse.

But the Council was in a hurry.

Then there was Siraj-ud-dowla's own equivocal behaviour. William Watts had enclosed in his report a letter from the Nawab which was strangely conciliatory, even whining. It was addressed to Pigot in person.

The Nawab began by saying that he had no intention of depriving the Company of its right to trade. It was all the fault of that 'very wicked and unruly man' Roger Drake who had apparently refused to hand over a refugee from the Nawab's entourage. The Governor, by inference, was entirely to blame. Watts was a 'Helpless poor and innocent man', while Pigot himself was a 'Substantial Person'. Hence the reason the Nawab had written about Drake's 'shameless and wicked Proceedings'.

It looked as though the Nawab, despite his success, was afraid. Certainly Aliverdi Khan's widow had warned him that no good would come of any hasty move, and by attacking the friends (and source of income) of the powerful Marwaris he was adding to the long list of those who might like to see him replaced.

In all the haste and excitement the Council forgot, whether on purpose or not, to inform Aldercron even of the fall of Calcutta, let alone their plans or retrieving it. He heard of it all at second-hand and on 21 August wrote a furious letter to the Council beginning: 'Both myself and every officer under my Command have more than once thought themselves greatly aggriev'd by your Conduct towards them.' Not even telling him that Calcutta has fallen seemed inconceivable. More precious days were lost in argument.

Clive in the meantime had arrived in Madras, and was as eager as George Pigot to get started.

But trouble now came once more from Watson. The Council, disgusted by Roger Drake's flight from Calcutta, had decided that when the Company got its property back, a new Council nominated by them would be installed at Fort William. Watson, who disliked getting mixed up with the in-fighting in the East India Company, declared that he would only sail if the intention were to restore and not replace the Calcutta Council.

For the sake of his co-operation the Madras Council agreed to reinstate Roger Drake, when – and if – the time came.

Meanwhile the Council wrote to Aldercron on 3 September asking for the 39th Foot to be allowed to go to Bengal (without, of course, Aldercron in command).

By 8 September, as there had been no reply, George Pigot wrote again asking for a reply to his previous letter.

Aldercron replied on 9 September, saying that he could not give an answer until he had called a Council of War, and that he could not do this at the moment 'by reason of the indisposition of my Lieutenant-Colonel and the absence of my Major'.

The frustration and anger at Aldercron's crude, but successful attempts at blocking the expedition were almost unbearable. If the expedition did not get off before the monsoon broke, Watson's squadron would have, for safety's sake, to leave the coast whether they went to Bengal or not. This was no doubt what Aldercron hoped would happen.

Eventually, after further days of argument, Aldercron agreed to allow 250 men of the 39th Foot to accompany the expedition, but only on condition that they were declared 'marines' for the operation and came under Watson's and Clive's command. He was adamant, however, over the artillery. None of it was to go. So the guns, ammunition and stores which had already been loaded on to ships, were carefully disembarked.

The Board, in London, was kept aware of these events, but only on an information basis. One of the oddest aspects of all the operations in India at this time was that events of enormous potential importance were being decided by relatively young men of junior rank. Clive was only thirty-two. He was still a Covenanted Servant of the East India Company at an official salary of £100 a year. Pigot was only a few years older, at a salary of £200. Nor were the rest of the Council, apart from Stringer Lawrence, any older. It was perhaps their youthfulness and vigour that made it possible for them to overcome the delaying tactics of Watson and Aldercron.

At last, on 16 October 1756, almost two months after the arrival of Watts's report and nearly four after the fall of Calcutta, the expedition finally set sail. There were five of the King's ships, and five belonging to the East India Company. On board were 900 Europeans and 1,500 sepoys. Five hundred more sepoys fron Bombay were expected to join them later on.

They had hardly started before the monsoon broke, and a wild north-easterly wind struck the convoy, making its progress so slow and painful that a further two months were spent in covering the six hundred-odd nautical miles between Madras and Bengal.

They reached Fulta, a village on the left bank of the Hooghli about twenty miles in a direct line south of Calcutta, but forty by the twisting river, on 22 December 1756. Here they met the fugitives from Calcutta, who had been reorganised by Kilpatrick a few weeks earlier.

Here, too, they learnt that news had been received in November that war had indeed broken out again between France and England. It was to be known, in history, as the Seven Years' War.

Two of the ships, the *Cumberland,* a 74-gunner, and the *Marlborough,* an East Indiaman, were delayed by the storm and still out at sea. On board the *Cumberland* were the 250

English soldiers of the 39th Foot, while the *Marlborough* carried 430 sepoys and most of the artillery.

But Clive was in favour of advancing as quickly as possible, and asked Watson to continue on the Baj-baj (Budge-Budge), some ten miles from Calcutta. Although Watson was prepared to bombard Baj-baj from the river, he insisted that the troops should be disembarked at Mayapur, some miles from the fort.

They left Mayapur at four in the afternoon and made through swamps and jungles for Baj-baj. The conditions were appalling. Huge palm trees with smooth grey boles towered above the jungle. Muddy rivers cut across the path. Trees, rotting in the damp excessive heat, lay at all angles. Thick creepers hung in festoons and had to be cut away. Here and there strange deserted temples, covered in the grey green of jungle growth, appeared suddenly in a clearing.

The air rustled and echoed with the chatter of monkeys. Hogs hurtled crazily across their path, squeaking as they scuttled for safety. In the open spaces gazelles, sensing the soldiers' approach, looked up fearfully and bounded gracefully away in the shimmering heat. And all the time, the mosquitoes danced and bit.

It was no better when night came on. The noises changed; that was all. Weird calls that sounded half human, echoed from the sweaty gloom. It was as if their progress was being noted by a thousand witnesses, and the news of their advance conveyed before them.

They marched all night, arriving sixteen hours later, exhausted, at the fort.

Though ill, Clive pushed forward his grenadier company and all the sepoys he had. The rest he held in reserve.

As far as he knew, the only enemy were those in the fort.

Suddenly, without warning, an infantry force of between two and three thousand men under the command of Monichund, whom Siraj-ud-dowla had made Governor of Calcutta, attacked.

There was a moment of confusion and near-panic.

Despite his fatigue and ill-health, Clive rallied his men and repulsed the attack, noting with satisfaction that Monichund himself received a shot in his turban.

In the meantime, Watson was bombarding the fort, and Captain Coote had landed with a company of King's Troops from the flagship. Coote was a thin handsome man with a great deal more charm of manner than was usual among military officers of the time. But he hid behind the charm the great courage and tenacity that was one day to make him Sir Eyre Coote.

At this time, however, he was a fairly junior officer with twelve years' service in the Army. Like Watson, and the rest of the regular officers, he had a certain inborn contempt for that amateur Lieutenant-Colonel Clive who was nominally, at least, his superior. He very much wanted to show that he, as a regular officer, was more than a match for Clive, and therefore marched rapidly and forcibly on the fort.

But this first moment of glory was taken away from him by a drunken sailor called Strahan. Strahan, who had been celebrating too liberally the conclusion, at last, of the storm-ridden journey from Madras, marched in a drunken haze alone on the fort. Protected, no doubt, by the God of Drunkards and moving blindly to a breach, he entered the fort brandishing a pistol. Seeing a group of defenders sitting near by and gazing at him in astonishment, he shouted 'the Fort is mine!' and gave himself three cheers.

Recovering from their surprise, the defenders attacked him; but, furious now at this unfriendly reception, he fought back indomitably, until a group of English soldiers came to his help.

The story soon got around, and Coote was furious at being balked by such a man.

The next day, Strahan was up before the Admiral on a charge of behaviour prejudicial to the good name of the Navy.

Strahan who, now sober, considered himself a hero, replied indignantly in answer to a question from Watson:

'Why, to be sure, sir, it was I who took the fort, but I hope there was no harm in it?'

He received a severe rebuke from the Admiral, and the threat of future punishment.

As the bewildered and indignant 'hero' left the room, he muttered: 'I'll never take another fort by myself as long as I live, by God!'

Perhaps that explains why, some years later when he was retired and living on a pension, he called upon the ship's surgeon, Edward Ives, and asked him to find him a job as a cook on a ship. That, he explained modestly, had always been his real ambition.

In the meantime, the army moved on Calcutta. Fort William was captured without a fight on 2 January 1757 by Captain Coote. Watson had instructed Coote not to deliver up his command unless on orders from the Admiral himself.

Coote was to interpret these orders literally.

On the morning after the enemy had evacuated Calcutta, Clive came to Fort William to take over as Governor, only to find himself face to face with Coote and his company of King's Troops. To Clive's anger and amazement, Coote, a captain, informed him that Admiral Watson had appointed him Governor of Fort William instead of Clive.

Clive immediately got in touch with the Admiral and asked for an explanation. Watson sent one of his captains, Speke, to Clive and informed him that unless he left the fort at once he, Watson, would open fire on him.

Thus it looked for a moment as if the naval commander-in-chief was about to do battle with army commander-in-chief.

But Clive, although reputedly often short-tempered and overbearing, could keep as cool in the face of his own side as in the face of the enemy. With considerable self-restraint, he agreed that Coote should remain in possession of the Fort William that day, on condition that it was returned to its proper owners, the East India Company, the next day.

Watson agreed, and war between the two commanders-in-chief was averted.

It was the old trouble. Like Aldercron, Watson could not, or would not, accept the fact that an officer in the East India Company could be superior in rank to a regular officer. Coote was a captain in the regular army. Clive held only the courtesy rank of Lieutenant-Colonel. Unlike Aldercron, however, Watson was efficient and forceful once he had made up his mind. Clive never had cause to complain of Watson's military support.

Clive had, anyhow, other matters to worry about. Once Calcutta was made safe again, the members of the East India Company who had run away so fast in June now returned with equal speed. This time they brought with them long claims for damages, a cry for revenge and the determination to make up for the money they had lost as quickly as possible.

Their selfishness and greed disgusted Clive.

He wrote to George Pigot complaining that '. . . the loss of private property, and the means of recovering it, seem to be the only object which take up the attention of the Bengal gentlemen.' At the same time, these 'Bengal gentlemen' were so dissatisfied with Clive's lack of enthusiasm for their complaints that they tried to get him to resign as Governor. A request that Clive turned down with his usual abruptness.

He could see beyond the narrow need of restoring private property. He knew that if the East India Company were to continue to operate in Bengal, it would have to come to a settlement with the Nawab, either by negotiation or by force.

The Nawab, too, was in a dilemma. His loss of revenue since the destruction of the East India Company was enormous. At the same time, he had lost the support of the bania families. His own subjects complained at the loss of trade. Even his army was discontented. He would have welcomed a new treaty with the English.

But, under the insistence of the returned merchants, an attack was planned on Hooghli, twenty miles further up river. Coote and Kilpatrick were in command of the land forces. A twenty-gun sloop and three other vessels accompanied the force. Although the sloop ran aground on a sand-bank and delayed the attack for five days, the expedition was successful, even though the prize-money, £15,000, was not considerable.

Revenge had been taken but, more important still, it was hoped that this show of strength would impress the Nawab.

It did indeed.

Siraj-ud-dowla had very naïve views about the strength of Europe. He believed quite sincerely that there were no more than ten thousand people at the most in Europe, and that the majority of these were weak and feeble.

His easy conquest of Calcutta had confirmed him in this opinion.

He had been alarmed and amazed at the ease with which Clive and Watson had recaptured Calcutta. But now, not content with this, it seemed that they were planning to invade the whole of Bengal. It was even said that they were planning to march on Dacca the capital of Eastern Bengal. From his capital, Moorshedabad, two hundred miles away, the Nawab watched these developments carefully. Fury and fear alternated in the mind of the indecisive Nawab. While wishing to sign a new treaty, he could not let this direct challenge to his authority go unpunished. Unlike the fighting in the Carnatic, this was not a question of one Indian prince against another. Here a despised commercial company was actually threatening his very existence.

He immediately raised a large army of 20,000 horsemen and 30,000 infantry and marched once again on Calcutta. Clive had at his disposition the 250 men of the 39th Foot, 750 of the Company's European troops and 1,500 sepoys; 2,000 against 50,000.

While advancing, Siraj-ud-dowla kept up his negotiation with Clive for a peaceful solution to the problem. Clive, who wanted to get back to Madras as soon as possible, carried on negotiating; but, like Watson, placed very little confidence in the Nawab's word.

By 4 February 1757, the Nawab was at the gates of Fort William itself, and was threatening to cut off Clive's small force altogether.

Clive sent two messengers to Siraj-ud-dowla saying that if the Nawab were genuine in his desire for a peaceful outcome, he could best show this by withdrawing from the Company's property. Siraj-ud-dowla, however, hardly bothered to see the messengers. They were lucky to get back alive.

This was enough for Clive. Far from being genuine in his desire for peace, the Nawab was using the negotiating period to strengthen his position and weaken Clive's. Already many of Clive's workmen, coolies and servants were deserting him, trade was at a standstill again, and he could only get provisions by river.

He asked Admiral Watson for reinforcements and ammunition, and that rough seaman, as usual when a real crisis was afoot, forgot old enmities and sent the reinforcements immediately.

Clive attacked at three a.m. the next morning.

There was the usual thick mist. The attack was a complete surprise, and had the mists lifted, as they normally did at eight, success would have been decisive.

But that day the mists did not lift; and in the subsequent confused fighting Clive lost 120 Europeans and 100 sepoys, as well as two guns, a very heavy loss for such a small army as his.

But the Nawab's losses were far heavier. More to the point, Siraj-ud-dowla also lost his nerve. The next morning he withdrew, and asked to sign a treaty of mutual friendship with the English. Watson advised Clive not to do this; but Clive, afraid that, if the Nawab were pushed to the point of despair, he might join up with the powerful French forces at Chandernagore, agreed.

A treaty restoring the East India Company to its earlier position in Calcutta, and agreeing in addition to compensation for damage, was signed on 9 February 1757. A second treaty of mutual aid, where each side agreed to come to the assistance of the other in the event of attack, was signed on 12 February 1757.

Chapter 10

From Chandernagore to Forgery

To Clive, the main enemy was, and always had been, the French. As long as de Bussy held power in Hyderabad, the East India Company, and through it English power, could never be safe. De Bussy could march south towards the Carnatic or north-east towards Bengal. He was already within 250 miles of Calcutta, having gained control of the Northern Circars, the stretch of coast line that joined Bengal to the Coromandel Coast.

If he could join Renault, the Governor of Chandernagore, the whole of Bengal would come under French control. The recent treaty signed with the Nawab would be immediately revoked, for Clive knew that it was only fear that had made Siraj-ud-dowla sign at all.

In the meantime, Watson had received orders from England to capture Chandernagore.

He and Clive were therefore in agreement on the need to attack.

The problem was: Would 'Sir Roger Dowler' stick to the treaty he had just signed with Clive, or would he come to the help of the French, with whom he had also, in fact, a general treaty of understanding and protection?

In a private letter to Payne, Chairman of the Court of Directors, Clive wrote: 'Our design upon Chandernagore is uncertain. I cannot yet fathom the Nabob's [Nawab's] sentiments.'

Both he and Watson felt that it was essential to get the Nawab's agreement before attacking Chandernagore. The French were strong, the fort well protected. The English were relatively weak. There was a difficult river passage to negotiate. If Siraj-ud-dowla came to the help of the French, there would be little chance of taking the place.

William Watts, by one of those somersaults that seemed common at the time, was now installed as an honorary prisoner and Company representative at Moorshedabad, and was very close to the Nawab. He was told to get the young ruler's agreement.

But to make things more complicated, the Nawab was being threatened by his own side, and by no less a person than the son of the Emperor at Delhi himself, the future Shah Alam, who was reputed to be advancing from Patna with a large force.

Admiral Watson was also trying to get the Nawab's permission to attack Chandernagore. In a letter in early March 1757, he tried persuasion, promising English help against the Emperor's son in return for the Nawab's permission: '. . . Monsieur Bussy is coming here with a great army. Is it to attack you? Is it to attack us? You are going to Patna. You ask our assistance. Can we, with the least degree of prudence, march with you, and leave our enemies behind us? You will then be too far off to support us, and we shall be unable to defend ourselves. Think what can be done in this situation. I see but one way. Let us take Chandernagore, and secure ourselves from any apprehensions from that quarter; and then we will assist you with every man in our power, and go with you, even to Delhi, if you will.'

A few days later, Watson learnt that far from helping the English, the Nawab was negotiating with the French, and had promised to send some of his own troops, ostensibly to the Governor of Hooghli, but in reality to be ready to support Renault in Chandernagore.

Watson immediately wrote a fiery letter of threats that ended: '. . . I will kindle such a flame in your country, as all the water in the Ganges shall not be able to extinguish. Farewell! remember that he who promises you this never yet broke his word with you or with any man whatsoever.'

Threatened on all sides, Siraj-ud-dowla wavered again.

He did not exactly give his permission, but nor did he withhold it and the patient William Watts informed Clive on 10 March 1757 that '. . . the Nawab has given his verbal consent for attacking Chandernagore'.

'Sir Roger Dowler' would have done better either to have supported the French full-heartedly, or the English. But he was bound by two contrary treaties, threatened both by Delhi and his own supporters. He just had not the ability to see where lay his true interest, nor the strength of character to carry a decision to its logical conclusion.

In the meantime, the reinforcements from Bombay had arrived, as well as the 74-gun *Cumberland* which had been held up by storms on the way up from Madras.

The attack on Chandernagore began.

Clive demanded its surrender on 13 March 1757. This was rejected by the French Governor.

The fort was fortified both on the land and the river side. It was defended by 500 French troops and 700 sepoys. It had plenty of guns and ammunition. The river leading to it was blocked by sunken vessels.

Or, at least, it was supposed to be.

But the French engineer in charge of the blocking operation left a narrow passage through the block-ships and then, deserting to the English, showed how Admiral Watson's ships could get through.

Once through, they moored up so close to the fort as to be within musket-fire of the defenders. The flagship alone was holed more than a hundred times and every officer except one was killed or wounded. The French fought with extreme gallantry and did not yield until the walls were rubble and all the guns destroyed.

In the meantime, Clive was attacking from the land side.

After more fierce fighting Chandernagore was finally captured on 23 March 1757. The English casualties had been higher than the French: 206 to 150. There were nearly 400 French prisoners, among them 60 French ladies. Clive and Watson made sure that they were made as comfortable as possible: 'their clothes, their linen, and everything have been suffered to go out.' Gallantry was upheld even in the fircest of fighting.

Clive, in his report to George Pigot at Fort St George, at Madras, wrote: 'You will observe the surrender is made to Admiral Watson; but common report will be just in publishing how great a share the land forces had in its conquest!'

Nevertheless, he always acknowledged the Admiral's courage. Later, in a report to the House of Commons, he stated 'that Admiral Watson's fleet surmounted difficulties which he believes no other ships could have done, and that it was impossible for him to do the officers of the squadron justice on that occasion.'

The slights at Fort William were forgotten, at least for the time being.

With Chandernagore captured, it might have been supposed that Clive and Watson could now return to Madras. They were urgently needed, as de Bussy was heading for Pondicherry. Stringer Lawrence, encumbered with Aldercron, would have a hard time defending Madras.

But in a private letter, dated 29 March 1757, Clive stated that Chandernagore was more important than Pondicherry; and that although he longed to be back in Madras, where, in addition to everything else, his wife was staying with Mrs Watson, the Admiral's wife, he would have to stay in Bengal now until August in order to settle matters with the Nawab.

Remembering the journey out, and the fact that the monsoon would begin again in June, he added: 'The lateness of the season makes the passage now very uncertain; and the length of it would certainly cause the loss of a great part of our forces.'

The requests for his return to Madras became more urgent as the danger from the French increased. The accommodating Monsieur Godeheu had now been replaced as Governor of Pondicherry by the much more decisive and powerful Lally de Tollendal. A French fleet was expected at any minute. With memories of what happened when La Bourdonnais turned up off Madras in 1746, it is not surprising that Pigot wanted Clive and Watson back as quickly as possible.

But Clive always took the longer view. He was convinced that he could serve the company and his country better in Bengal than in Madras. He had no trust in the word of the weak and vacillating Nawab.

In a private letter to George Pigot, dated 30 April 1757, he wrote of the Nawab's behaviour: 'One day he tears up my letters, and turns out our vakeel [representative], and orders his army to march; he next countermands it, sends for the vakeel, and begs his pardon for what he has done. Twice a week he threatens to impale Mr Watts. . . .'

Siraj-ud-dowla was still negotiating with the French, still in touch with de Bussy, alternatively cursing the patient William Watts, and asking him to convey his compliments to Clive and Watson. In truth, the Nawab would have loved to have got rid of the English, but could think of no way of doing so. Instead of keeping the English in the subservient role of merchants as his grandfather had done, he was, by his very indecisiveness, forcing upon Clive a much more aggressive attitude.

Clive was concerned, too, about the actions of the East India Company's Calcutta Committee, or, as they liked to call themselves, the Select Committee. Unlike the strong Madras Committee, under the decisive control of George Pigot and Stringer Lawrence, the Calcutta Committee had been taken over again by the weak and self-seeking men who had fled so rapidly from Fort William the year before.

Clive felt that if he left Bengal now, Siraj-ud-dowla would regain courage, descend once more upon Calcutta, put the Select Committee to flight, and with French help push the East India Company out of Bengal for ever. The real beneficiaries of this would not be the Nawab himself, the merchants of Calcutta or the people of Bengal, but France, who would soon control the weak Nawab and add Bengal to Hyderabad and the Northern Circars.

Once again, it was a relatively junior officer who was

having to make strategic decisions that could affect his country's whole future. Decisions that should have been taken in Whitehall were, in fact, being taken in the hot pre-monsoon jungle in Bengal and a small fort on the Coromandel Coast between two men of strong character: Robert Clive and George Pigot.

It was at this point that Clive first heard that a conspiracy was being formed at the Nawab's court to get rid of the ruler.

The informant was William Watts; and his source was the ubiquitous Omi Chand.

Omi Chand appeared to be friends with everyone. When Siraj-ud-dowla took Calcutta, Omi Chand lost a good deal of money, yet it was said that he was somehow instrumental in getting Holwell and the survivors of the siege of Fort William into the Black Hole of Calcutta, as it was now firmly, if incorrectly, called. Later, it was on his estate that Siraj-ud-dowla encamped in his second attempt to capture Fort William. Now, he was conspiring against the Nawab.

The truth perhaps was that he was a man in love with money. The bania were all eager to make money, and did so; but, like Shylock, Omi Chand loved it for itself.

He himself was not involved directly with the conspiracy. As a Hindu, he would not be allowed to be one of the principals anyhow. The Mohammedans, however much they might quarrel amongst themselves, kept the positions of power to themselves.

The main conspirator was Mir Jaffar, the Nawab's uncle, one of his main generals and Commander-in-Chief at the capture of Fort William. Four-fifths of the army was, it was reported, ready to rebel against the Nawab. Had the future Shah Alam continued his advance into Bengal instead of accepting a large sum of money and returning to Delhi, Siraj-ud-dowla might have been deposed then and there.

But the withdrawal of the threat from Delhi, the presence of Law, who had been one of Dupleix's old generals at Trichinopoly, and the mysterious but threatening movements of de Bussy, gave the Nawab hope that even now the French would come to his rescue, and get rid of not only the English, but those of his own family, who might be conspiring against him.

As a precaution he moved his army to a small village called Plassey.

Clive, in the meantime, was certain that as long as Siraj-ud-dowla ruled, there would be no stability.

In the middle of April, he asked Watson for his help; but Watson, though threatening the Nawab by letter, could offer no concrete help. The river made it impossible for his squadron to operate. The Select Committee were as unhelpful as ever.

The Nawab, still distracted by his two agreements, complained to Watts that though he had allowed the English to take Chandernagore and ordered the French out of his country (he did not add that he had told the French to stay), Clive, whom he called Sabut Jung ('daring in war'), and the Admiral, continually pestered him to take more action against the French. His patience was exhausted. He would march against Calcutta for a third time.

In fact, once again he wavered, and contented himself with forbidding stores and ammunition to be sent to a small detachment of English-trained sepoys at Cossimbazar, and threatening to cut off the ears and noses of anyone trying to get through.

Clive replied to this latest double-move by telling Watts on 23 April 1757: '. . . I cannot depend upon his friendship; and therefore shall get everything ready for a march.'

In the meantime, Mir Jaffar's conspiracy was progressing too. The plotters had at first chosen a powerful and wealthy Mohammedan called Lattee. Omi Chand knew him, and soon was a centre-piece of the intrigue.

But suddenly, without warning, the plotters switched to Mir Jaffar. In switching, they did not bother to inform Omi Chand of the change of candidate.

Omi Chand, like the rest of the Hindu merchants, never expected a Hindu to rule Bengal. They accepted that it would be a Mohammedan. It was just a question of which Mohammedan would treat them less harshly.

At the same time, the Mohammedan rulers preferred to employ Hindu merchants. For, as one of them put it: 'a Mohammedan was like a sieve – much of what was poured in went through; while a Hindu was like a sponge, which retained all, but on pressure gave back, as required, what it had absorbed.'

It just depended on how much the Mohammedan squeezed the Hindu sponge. The previous Nawab of Bengal, Aliverdi Khan, had been wise and cautious. He had squeezed his Hindu merchants as little as possible.

Siraj-ud-dowla, his grandson, was very different. From the first day of his rule, he had lived at a very high rate. Nothing was too expensive or grand for him. Money was laid out for every kind of luxury. In a time when vice and debauchery were commonplace, his debaucheries exceeded anything seen before. He had soon used up the reserves his frugal grandfather had accumulated.

To get more money, he squeezed the Hindu sponge mercilessly.

The Hindus retaliated by supporting the plotters. Though fearful of starting a rebellion themselves, they were always ready to help any change of ruler, if it meant alleviating their burdens.

But though subservient and devious, they had their pride. Omi Chand's pride was hurt by the casual way he had been treated by the conspirators. But he hid his resentment and spite, at least for the time being, and soon made himself as indispensible to Mir Jaffar as he had been to Lattee. He also gained, or regained, the confidence of the Nawab, and he acted as a go-between between Watts and Clive.

He thus became an essential link in the events that were taking shape; yet no one, except perhaps the foolish Nawab himself, really trusted Omi Chand. Mir Jaffar certainly didn't. Nor did Watts.

On 17 May, Watts reported that Omi Chand had gone to

the Nawab with an extraordinary story that the English and French had made it up; and that a combined Anglo-French army would soon attack the Nawab. For this breath-taking piece of fiction, the grateful Nawab agreed to pay Omi Chand £40,000.

However, this was nothing to what was to come next. The crafty Omi Chand went to William Watts and calmly told him that unless the conspirators agreed to pay him £300,000, he would reveal the whole conspiracy to Siraj-ud-dowla. He was being revenged for his slight as well as filling his pocket.

Clive, who until then had not fully shared Watt's distrust of the Hindu, was now completely convinced that Omi Chand was not only greedy, but a blackmailer.

He immediately decided to meet treachery with treachery. He could outsmart Omi Chand. The means were quite simple. The Hindu had insisted that a clause should be inserted in the treaty, which was being drawn up between the conspirators and the East India Company, stating that he should receive 'five per cent on all the Nabob's treasures and thirty lacs in money'. [The lac was worth £10,000.]

All right. His demands would be inserted in the treaty; but they would be on a false treaty, written on red paper. The real treaty, written on white paper would contain no mention of the deal.

The Select Committee hesitated, perhaps from scruples or fear; but were eventually won over by Clive, and signed the two documents.

Admiral Watson however was adamant. Nothing on earth would make him sign the false red treaty. He had never been in favour of the plan to depose the Nawab, mainly because he felt there weren't enough English troops to make it succeed. Though he promised to lend Clive 200 seamen, he had little hope of success. Besides, his instructions had been to capture Chandernagore. That had already been achieved.

He would not change his mind, even when Clive pointed out that Omi Chand would be suspicious if the Admiral had not signed the false document.

There was nothing else for it: Clive forged the Admiral's signature himself.

Chapter 11

Mir Jaffar's Treachery

The Gentlemen of Bengal's scruples over the way Omi Chand was to be treated did not last long. Even Admiral Watson's reservations were more a question of form than anything: he was quite prepared to share in any plunder that might be available.

In cash alone, the new Nawab, if successfully installed on Siraj-ud-dowla's throne, would be expected to make good the Company's losses in Calcutta, estimated at a million pounds. In addition, £500,000 were to be distributed to private European claimants, £200,000 to local, mainly Hindu inhabitants and £70,000 to the Armenian merchants who had also lost their property. Half a million pounds were to be shared by the Army and the Navy, and a further £120,000 to be doled out as a special sweetener to the members of the Select Committee.

There were also to be large land concessions in and around Calcutta, where rents could be collected directly by the East India Company, and all operational expenses of the English troops in support of the pretender to be met.

No wonder the scruples of the various contestants did not last long.

Clive seems never to have had any at all.

Sending the two treaties to Watts at Moorshedabad, he wrote on 19 May 1757: '. . . both the admirals and gentlemen agree that Omichund [sic] is the greatest villain upon earth; and that now he appears in the strongest light, what he was always suspected to be, a villain in grain. However to counterplot this scoundrel, and at the same time to give him no room to suspect our intentions, enclosed you will receive two forms of agreement; the one real, to be strictly kept by us; the other fictitious. In short, this affair concluded, Omichund will be treated as he deserves. This you will acquaint Meer Jaffier with.'

Omi Chand was shown the red treaty. The wily old Hindu inspected it carefully, noted the signatures and said he was satisfied.

Watts suggested that, for safety's sake, Omi Chand should now go to Calcutta. Scrafton, Clive's private secretary, would accompany him.

Omi Chand hesitated. He had still only been paid half the promised forty thousand pounds by the Nawab for the false news about the Anglo-French rapprochement.

Watts and Scrafton between them, however, managed to persuade the old man that his life was in danger, as indeed all of their lives were, and he agreed to leave Moorshedabad.

Then commenced what must have been one of the most curious journeys in history. On the one side Clive's earnest young secretary, on the other the suspicious and avaricious Hindu.

At Cossimbazar, shortly after leaving the capital, he was found to be missing.

Scrafton immediately sent out a search party.

The indefatigable old man was discovered closeted with the Nawab's treasurer trying, unsuccessfully, even now, to get the rest of the forty thousand pounds.

Once more they set off, once again Omi Chand disappeared.

This time, when he reappeared, he told Scrafton that he had been to see his old friend Roydullab at Plassey.

Roydullab was also one of the conspirators, and having seen the white, or real treaty, told Omi Chand that the Hindu banker's name was not in it.

What, he demanded suspiciously, had Scrafton to say to that?

Scrafton kept his sang-froid, and retorted that naturally, as the treaty was secret, details of this kind would not have been communicated to a junior conspirator like Roydullab.

Omi Chand was once again satisfied.

The party arrived safely at Calcutta, where Omi Chand, in order to lull his suspicions completely, was given an enormously friendly welcome. When it came to double-crossing, the Gentlemen of Bengal were as adept as any Eastern merchant. They and Omi Chand must have spent some remarkable evenings of mutual congratulation together.

In the meantime, news was received on 12 June 1757 that Mir Jaffar had signed the treaty.

Clive, his quarrel with Watson and Coote a forgotten event of the past, now set off eagerly.

He commanded an 'army' of approximately 3,200 men. Of these, 900 were English, 200 were Eurasian and 2,100 sepoys. He had eight six-pounders and two small howitzers. He had no cavalry whatsoever.

The Nawab on the other hand could count on a nominal army of 50,000. It consisted of 35,000 infantry and 15,000 cavalry. He had 53 heavy calibre guns, and a useful nucleus of 50 Frenchmen under the command of the energetic Monsieur St Frais, who had been a member of the French Council at Chandernagore.

All depended upon whether Mir Jaffir kept to the treaty he had signed with the English.

Clive, who until then, had been writing conciliatory letters to the Nawab, now altered the tone completely. He wrote what was virtually a declaration of war.

He was then at Chandernagore. Leaving a hundred of Admiral Watson's seamen there to guard the place, he set off immediately, the Europeans, artillery and stores travelling by boat, the sepoys overland.

On 13 June 1757, William Watts escaped from Moorshedabad, and joined Clive at Cutna.

He assured Clive that Mir Jaffar would not weaken.

Clive pushed on up the right bank of the Hooghli. He halted on the 16th at Patlee. Whilst there he sent Coote with a detachment to capture Cutna Fort. This Coote succeeded in doing on the 17th.

The army marched on and encamped on the plain outside Cutna, on the right bank of the Hooghli, fifteen miles fron Plassey.

On 19 June the monsoon broke. It seemed as if the whole sky were falling upon them, turning the pale earth to mud. Their flimsy tents were useless. The whole army took shelter in the huts and small houses in the town, thankful to get out of the deluge for a while at least.

Clive was a very worried man. It had been agreed that Mir Jaffar and his troops would join Clive at Cutna. But instead, Mir Jaffar, playing for safety, had merely sent Clive a letter saying that he would join him 'on the field of battle.'

It looked as though Mir Jaffar was preparing to double cross the conspirators.

Clive wrote, on 19 June 1757: '. . . I feel the greatest anxiety at the little intelligence I receive from Meer Jaffier; and, if he is not treacherous, his sangfroid or want of strength will, I fear, overset the expedition. I am trying a last effort, by means of a Brahmin, to prevail upon him to march out and join us. I have appointed Plassey the place of rendez-vous. . . .'

If, he continued, Mir Jaffar did not respond, then he, Clive, would halt the army. He would not risk it unnecessarily. There was enough captured grain in Cutna to keep the army going during the rainy season. Their presence there might force the Nawab to agree to favourable terms. Alternatively, when the monsoon was over, the Nawab's many enemies both within and without the country might combine to overthrow him.

Two days later, on 21 June 1757, Clive held his first and only Council of War.

The proposal put to it was: 'Whether in our present situation, without assistance, and on our own bottom, it would be prudent to attack the Nabob [Nawab]; or whether we should wait till joined by some country power?'

There were sixteen members in the Council of War. Nine

including Clive and Kilpatrick, voted against an immediate attack. Seven, led by Coote, voted to continue the advance.

As soon as the meeting was over, Clive went off on his own to consider the position.

Whilst he stood, in a grove, wondering whether the Council of War, a means of action alien to his nature, had come to the right conclusion, he received a further message, presumably via the accommodating Brahmin mentioned earlier, from Mir Jaffar.

In it, Mir Jaffar said that although he could not come to Cutna, he would bring his army over to Clive's side once the English commander had covered the fifteen miles that separated them.

Clive realised that Mir Jaffar was, in fact, challenging him. He, Mir Jaffar, would only abandon the Nawab if Clive made an almost impossible display of audacity. Even Clive 'the Daring in War' might hesitate, with little more than three thousand men, in attacking an army of fifty thousand. If he did, then he saw quite clearly that there might be no rebellion at all.

Already a huge number of people knew about it. The only person who didn't seemed to be the Nawab himself, or if he had heard rumours, he had dismissed them. But if he were really made to believe in the existence of the plot, Mir Jaffar and the rest would soon be dead. Sirja-ud-dowla added a nice streak of sadism to his weakness and indecisiveness.

If Mir Jaffar's revolt failed, there would probably never be another chance of getting rid of the tiresome young ruler. De Bussy was still within striking distance. If Siraj-ud-dowla were strengthened with a really first-class corps of French troops, no one, not even the Mahrattas or the Emperor at Delhi, could dislodge him.

Clive returned from the grove. His mind was made up. Without consulting anybody else, he reversed the decision of the Council of War. The advance would continue the next morning.

The monsoon had made the land soggy and glutinous, the

river fast running and difficult to navigate. But the next morning the small army marched to the Bhaghirathi river, and crossed it the same afternoon.

There was no enemy opposition.

But there was plenty from the elements. The rain came down in the usual monsoon torrents. Just as he had done on the march to Arcot, so now Clive led his men on without a break towards Plassey, fifteen miles up stream. The mud was appalling. The going heavy as a nightmare. In addition the boats had to be dragged against the fast-moving current.

They struggled on all night through the mud and torrents, and reached Plassey at one in the morning, wet and exhausted.

Mir Jaffar had told Clive that the Nawab intended to spend the night at Mankarah, three miles north of Plassey. But, as in so many matters, his information was not reliable. For Siraj-ud-dowla changed his mind and encamped within a mile of Plassey.

Clive's weary troops made for a mango grove beside the river, half a mile north of Plassey; so that they were, in fact, within five hundred yards of the Nawab's outposts.

The beating of drums and cymbals, and the sounding of clarions showed where the enemy was situated.

Clive immediately put out pickets and sentries. Despite the noise, the torrential rain and the closeness of the Nawab's army, the exhausted men got two or three hours sleep.

They were awakened at four a.m. and stood to in readiness for the Nawab's expected attack.

Clive had chosen his position well. The mango grove was eight hundred yards long and three hundred wide. A wall and a ditch protected the front and right-hand sides. The left was protected by the river and a hunting lodge. Behind was the village. It was almost a fort.

Yet, when at day-break the rain had lifted and he looked over the mud ramparts, even he must have been astounded at the sight that met his eyes.

Immediately to the front, not more than five hundred

yards away, were the French with their guns. Behind them, line upon line of Indian troops stood at the ready. Behind them again could be seen the tents of the Nawab's camp.

But this was only a small part of the Nawab's army. The major part was spread across the plain in a huge semi-circle that stretched from the river bend almost to Plassey which lay behind him.

In all, some fifty-five thousand men, were poised to swoop down on the three thousand men in the mud-walled mango grove.

There were forty thousand infantry. Some were armed with guns, some with bows, arrows, spears. The fifteen thousand cavalrymen were particularly impressive. They were in fact Pathans, born soldiers, skilful and brave. Both their horses and equipment were magnificent, far superior to anything that Clive had encountered in the Carnatic.

Along the whole of this huge semi-circle the heavy calibre guns, mounted on platforms, were dragged by teams of white oxen and pushed by elephants. The noise of drums and bugles, and the shouting of men, was continuous.

By contrast, Clive's small force was utterly silent. The English were, for the most part, battle-trained and hardened. The 250 men Aldercron had so reluctantly allowed to accompany the expedition as 'marines' formed the core. To this day, the successors to the 39th Foot carry the battle honour 'Plassey' with – as they were the first regular troops to see action in India – the added motto 'Primus in Indis'. The Eurasians and sepoys were equally battle trained, self-confident and calm. In Clive, Kilpatrick and Coote they had leaders they trusted.

In the Nawab's army, huge as it was, there was no trust either between the soldiers and their generals, between the generals themselves, or between them and the Nawab. The French, it was true, were determined and well-led, but there were at the most only fifty of them. For the rest, there were nothing but doubts, suspicions and the deliberate ignoring of orders.

Two of the main commanders, Roydullab and Mir Jaffar, were members of the conspiracy. Indeed, when ordered to attack, they made one excuse after another, in order to delay the moment of decision. Only one man, Mir Mudin, commanding the Nawab's right flank, was really prepared to fight for Siraj-ud-dowla.

But if Mir Jaffar deliberately misunderstood the Nawab's orders, he did not, as he had promised, come over to Clive, but remained tantalisingly immobile out in the plain, waiting for the outcome of the battle.

Chapter 12

The Astonishing Victory at Plassey

The sun shone down on the hot steamy plain.

The battle opened with almost every gun of the Nawab's artillery firing into the grove. Cannon-balls, weighing any- thing from nine to thirty-two pounds each, hurtled through the humid air to land on the mud walls, or the trees beyond.

Surprisingly little damage was done.

'The Daring in War' might take enormous strategical and tactical risks, but he never risked a man's life unnecessarily. He gave instructions that his men were not to show them- selves, but were to remain spaced behind the wall. In this way the cannon-balls sailed harmlessly overhead, or buried themselves in the wall itself.

On the other hand, there was little he could do in reply. His eight guns were six-pounders. They were out of range of the Nawab's much heavier guns. Even if they had been able to reach the enemy artillery, they would not have done much damage.

He therefore, as he reported later, decided to remain 'quiet in front, in hopes of a successful attack on their camp at night.'

He was more bothered by the fifty Frenchmen along the river immediately in front of him than by anything else. St Frais had moved up to a reservoir protected by mud walls only a few hundred yards in front of the hunting lodge. With him were two heavy guns.

The fire from these two guns was both accurate and intense. Had it not been for the mud wall there would have been many casualties.

Just before eleven o'clock, after three to four hours'

bombardment, Mir Mudin, attacked with five thousand infantry and seven thousand cavalry. But despite the personal bravery of Mir Mudin himself, the attack was disorganised and ill-directed.

No breach had been made in the walls, and, as attacks on fortified places had for centuries always been aimed at a breach, the advancing hordes seemed lost and indecisive. They circled about, within a few hundred yards of the grove, as if looking for somewhere to attack. or hoping that their presence and noise would stampede the defenders.

This was the opportunity Clive's small artillery force had been waiting for.

The six-pounders fired continuously into the packed ranks of the attackers. Every shot, perfectly aimed and controlled, found its target. Men began to fall by the dozen. Among them was the faithful Mir Mudin, mortally wounded.

With his fall panic seems to have taken hold of the attackers. They streamed back to the encampment, leaving only Monsieur St Frais and his men tenaciously firing at the English.

Out on the plain itself Roydullab and Mir Jaffar maintained their masterly immobility.

But the Nawab's heavy guns still kept firing. That is until the rain started again. The powder was badly soaked and the fuses too wet to light. The guns stopped firing.

This was the moment that Clive imagined the Nawab's cavalry would attack.

For, as he remarked, '. . . we imagined the horse would now, if ever, have attacked in the hopes of breaking us, as they might have thought we could not then make use of our firelocks; but their ignorance or the brisk fire of our artillery prevented them from attempting it.'

The smaller English guns and their more highly trained gunners had not been affected by the heavy rain. Clive had had the forethought to have them covered.

Clive, with that sureness of the commander who is in complete control, now realised that it was just a question of waiting for the right opportunity to occur. It might be that Mir Jaffar would finally make up his mind, that the Nawab would attack once more, or that both sides would wait for the terrible rain to lift, or night, with its opportunities, to come on.

Nothing, he thought, was likely to happen for an hour or so at least; for it was lunch-time, and Nawab's troops were in the habit of retiring into their camp to cook their midday meal.

Other great commanders before and after him have had the knack of instant controlled sleep. Curling up inside the hunting lodge, within a few hundred yards of the French guns, he fell immediately asleep.

He had given instructions that he was to be awakened an hour later.

When he was awakened he saw immediately that the situation had changed. Deprived of their heavy guns and the only active general, the Nawab's troops had not ventured out again.

Kilpatrick had also sensed this and had immediately got together an attacking party.

Clive forbade him to go forward. Kilpatrick was, after all, the army's second-in-command; and in battle the second-in-command's one and only responsibility was to keep alive, so that if the commander were killed or wounded there would be somebody fresh to take over.

However, Kilpatrick's idea was excellent.

Clive now sent forward a strong force supported by four field-guns under the command of Eyre Coote.

Their objective was the protected reservoir where the French, under St Frais, still remained with their guns.

The French fought with their usual gallantry and tenacity, but the fire of the English and the determined assault, particularly of the men of the 39th Foot, was decisive. By three o'clock the reservoir was captured.

In the meantime, Siraj-ud-dowla was beseeching Mir Jaffar to attack Clive and cut him off from his supplies and the river. But all Mir Jaffar and the other conspirators suggested was that Siraj-ud-dowla should withdraw his army to Mankarah and prepare to fight on the following day.

At almost the same time, he sent Clive a message saying that the English in turn should attack at three the next morning.

But Clive and events were moving faster than either Mir Jaffar or Sirja-ud-dowla realised.

Encouraged by this success, the English now moved on to a redoubt and a mound immediately at the gates of the Nawab's camp.

A last minute sortie was made by the troops still faithful to their young ruler; but without experienced commanders, with the cavalry all mixed up with the infantry, they were little more than excellent target practice for the gunners.

The redoubt and the mound were captured at 4.30 p.m. The Indian troops in the encampment now panicked completely, and abandoning arms, artillery and elephants fled northwards towards Moorshedabad.

Among them, on a camel, went Siraj-ud-dowla.

Clive's men pursued the disorganised enemy for six miles, but being without cavalry could not exploit the rout.

However, an enormous amount of war material and stores had been captured. No less than forty guns had been abandoned. Thousands of bullock-drawn carts loaded with baggage of all kinds were taken. Nothing was left of Siraj-ud-dowla's army except Mir Jaffar's troops who, apart from an occasional pretence-sortie, had taken no part whatsoever in the fighting.

Indeed, Plassey was, from the military point of view, almost a non-battle. The greater part of the combatants, particularly on the Nawab's side, played no active role at all. Most of the cavalry remained immobile. Only a portion of the infantry attacked. Even on the English side the infantry, apart from Eyre Coote's attack, was hardly engaged.

Casualties were astonishingly small: twenty-two killed and fifty wounded on the English side; five hundred killed and wounded on the Nawab's. Rarely has so decisive a battle been won at such little cost.

It was essentially an artillery battle; but an artillery battle where the normal rules were reversed. The heavier guns, with the longer range, generally have the advantage. The side with the greatest number of guns usually wins.

But though Clive's artillery was out-gunned six-to-one in numbers and five-to-one in weight of cannon-balls, and was, for the most part, out of range of the opposing artillery, he won. Indeed, the very lightness of his guns was to his advantage. The heavy ox-drawn, elephant-pushed guns of the Nawab were unwieldy and unmanoeuvrable. Clive could rush his light guns quickly to where they were needed. Then again, the heavy cannon-balls of the thirty-two pounders, lobbed inaccurately into the grove did very little damage, but the grape-shot of the six-pounders fired at almost point-blank range into the milling crowds of the Nawab's semi-disorganised troops was deadly.

Beyond this, the battle was a psychological exercise in bluff. Right up to the end, Mir Jaffar's attitude was never defined. Clive knew that at the slightest sign of weakness, Mir Jaffar would have attacked; and with those superb Pathan horsemen at his disposal, the outcome would have been, to say the least, doubtful.

Only a continuous and excessive display of audacity would keep the shifty commander neutral, if not actively on Clive's side.

Clive had realised this after the Council of War. It had made him cross the river and advance at all speed to Plassey. It had dictated all his movements since his arrival. His alarm at Kilpatrick's projected sortie had been caused by his realisation that, had the sortie failed, and Kilpatrick's men been seen to withdraw, this would have been interpreted by Mir Jaffar as weakness. It might have been enough for that cautious traitor to turn on the conspirators and appear to his indecisive nephew as his liberator.

Hence, when Clive mounted the attack on the French

stronghold, he made sure that, on that limited front at least, he had the necessary tactical strength to succeed.

He realised that, at Plassey, it was not the relative strengths of the opposing armies that mattered, not the number of cavalry on one side or the lack of it on the other that counted, not the discrepancy between the fire-power that would be decisive, but his own personal conduct that would decide the issue.

He had earned for himself, in Indian eyes, by the defence of Arcot, the name of 'Daring in War'. Now, for Mir Jaffar's benefit, it was tested to the full. As usual, when faced with danger, Clive's cool courage was at its best.

He never gave Mir Jaffar the chance to double-cross him the way that Siraj-ud-dowla had done, for Clive was showing that he was more than a courageous leader, more than a sound tactician, more even than a far-seeing strategical general. He was demonstrating that he had that insight into human motives and reactions that is the basic of statesmanship.

He would have, in the days to come, much need of such qualities; for by the astonishing victory at Plassey he had transformed the struggling, often vacillating and undoubtedly self-seeking East India Company merchants in Calcutta into the virtual rulers of the whole of Bengal, a country larger and more heavily populated than England.

Chapter 13

Clive Kingmaker

Mir Jaffar and his somewhat truculent son, Miran, turned up the next day at Clive's camp at Daudpur, six miles beyond Plassey.

Mir Jaffar was not entirely at his ease.

He feared, not without reason, that Clive might be annoyed at the dilatory way the turn-coat Mohammedan had behaved the day before.

But Clive was not one to hold a grudge. He had wanted to overthrow Siraj-ud-dowla, and put Mir Jaffar on the throne. This looked now like being accomplished. The fact that Mir Jaffar had not done all he should was of little importance. More pertinent was it to get the new Nawab quickly to work.

So when Mir Jaffar came to him, Clive immediately greeted him with the title of Nawab, and said nothing at all about the day before.

Mir Jaffar, relieved and grateful, promised that he would stick by his agreement and do everything in his power to promote the prosperity of the East India Company.

After further exchanges of mutual admiration, Clive suggested that Mir Jaffar should march immediately upon Moorshedabad, so that the transistional period between him and Siraj-ud-dowla should be as brief and peaceful as possible.

Mir Jaffar agreed, and set off at once for Moorshedabad.

Clive took the precaution of sending his wife's brother-in-law Walsh forward with Watts, to keep an eye on Mir Jaffar, and find out what exactly was in the treasury.

In the meantime, Siraj-ud-dowla's fast camel had brought him safely to Moorshedabad.

Here he tried to decide what to do next. As usual, he asked opinion of those around him. The older and perhaps wiser men advised him to give himself up to the English. He would only be deposed and banished. He might even be given a sufficient 'retirement' pension to live moderately well outside Bengal.

Obsessed now with traitors, Siraj-ud-dowla considered this latest piece of advice to be the very essence of treachery. He refused even to consider the idea.

Others suggested that he should fortify Moorshedabad and fight the English.

This he found more attractive and gave orders that the army should stand and fight.

But hardly had he made this decision than he was told that it was Mir Jaffar, and not Clive, who was marching upon the city.

The young man gave up all pretence of courage. Only yesterday, when he had finally pleaded with Mir Jaffar for his help, he had taken off his turban and thrown it at the other's feet.

In the Mohammedan world this was the final act of humiliation, the complete abandonment of self, the last cry for help.

Mir Jaffar had sworn, again in the Mohammedan way, to defend the turban and its wearer to the death.

It was an oath that no Mohammedan broke. Yet Mir Jaffar had still not come to his help, had still gone over to the Nawab's enemies. Now he was marching on Moorshedabad at the head of his army.

There was no hope left.

Disguising himself as his own servant, taking only with him his favourite wife, one eunuch and a basket full of jewels hastily scooped up fron the palace treasury, the once all-powerful ruler fled from his capital, shortly after Mir Jaffar entered it from the other side. Clive followed Mir Jaffar to Moorshedabad on 29 June with a bodyguard of 200 English soldiers and 300 sepoys.

This somewhat large personal bodyguard was not there entirely to impress the inhabitants. Clive would probably have preferred to have entered the city in a much less ostentatious way. But the day before he had received news that Miran, Mir Jaffar's seventeen-year-old son, was plotting to assassinate him.

This was not as unbelievable as might be thought. Wholesale assassinations, both of the defeated and sometimes of the successful, often followed oriental revolutions.

Only eight years earlier, Muzzaffar Jang, the first Nizam to be put by Dupleix on the throne of Hyderabad, had been murdered on his way back from his coronation at Pondicherry.

Miran resembled Siraj-ud-dowla in that he combined a somewhat limited intelligence with a good deal of cruelty. Perhaps, too, he was jealous of Clive and ashamed that his father owed his elevation to a low foreign merchant.

Whatever the attitude of his son, there was no doubt about the gratitude of Mir Jaffar. He put one of the largest of the palaces at Moorshedabad at Clive's disposal. The garden alone was big enough to accommodate all five hundred of Clive's guard.

At his coronation that same evening, Mir Jaffar insisted that Clive should lead him to his throne, and only then would he accept the homage from the waiting nobles and courtiers.

Never in all Mohammedan history had a ruler been placed on his throne by a foreign merchant. Bemused and mesmerised, hardly able to believe what they saw, the erstwhile courtiers of Siraj-ud-dowla greeted their new ruler.

The next day Mir Jaffar and Clive called on Jagat Seth at the latter's palace at Moorshedabad. Jagat Seth was, like Omi Chand, a Marwari merchant. He was the first of many Marwari millionaires. He was the richest man in Moorshedabad, probably in Bengal, possibly in the whole of India. He had inspired the conspirators, his hatred for Siraj-ud-dowla dating back to the day that unstable young man had insulted him gratuitously. Now he had got his revenge.

They had a problem. Watts had calculated that there was at least four million pounds in Siraj-ud-dowla's treasury; but when an inventory was taken, it was found that there was only one and a half million. Perhaps Siraj-ud-dowla had spent the rest.

As the agreed share-out amongst the victors and the compensation to those who had lost so heavily when Calcutta had fallen amounted to two and a half million pounds, it was obvious that Mir Jaffar could not possibly pay it all.

The matter was put to Jagat Seth for a decision. He suggested that half should be paid immediately, two-thirds in cash, one-third in gold and silver plate, jewels and other goods. The remaining half should be paid in equal instalments over the next three years.

This was agreed by all concerned.

A hundred boats with flags flying sailed off down-stream laden with the treasure. The boats were greeted with cheers by the inhabitants of Calcutta, and compensation for loss was paid out almost at once.

Equally important, but more difficult to assess, was the value to the East India Company rents which the Company's servants could now collect from the 900 square miles around Calcutta.

In his report, Clive estimated it at £100,000 a year at least.

Everybody was now putting in a claim for a share of the spoils: East India Company Committee members, army officers, naval officers and Omi Chand, secure in the knowledge that by the signed red treaty he would receive, at his own calculation not less than £650,000.

Omi Chand, old but eager, came into Jagat Seth's large room where the conference was being held.

He listened quietly while the clauses in the white treaty were being read out. Shortly, he knew, the even more secret red one, the one in which his name figured so prominently, would be produced.

Clive, who had never learnt any Indian language, turned to Scrafton and said in English: 'It is now proper to undeceive Omi Chand. You may tell him how the case stands.'

Scrafton, the same man who had accompanied Omi Chand to Calcutta a few days earlier, now said in the language of the country, 'The red treaty is a sham: you are to have nothing.'

Omi Chand fell back as if he had been blasted by an explosion. One of his attendants jumped forward and caught him as he fell fainting. He was carried out to his palanquin, and taken home. Here he sat, motionless and wide-eyed, until those around watching this strange immobility thought he had gone out of his mind.

A miser, victim of his own greed, he had, like Shylock, lost all at the very moment of triumph.

Clive never had any sense of guilt about his actions. When, later, he was asked whether he would have acted the same way all over again, he replied: 'Yes, a hundred times over.' Omi Chand was not only unscrupulous, he was a blackmailer as well. However hard Clive could be, he held honour between friends to be sacred. He himself never forgot a friend, and often came to their help. Had Omi Chand merely demanded money, he would in all probability have, after argument, agreed a reasonable sum. It was the fact that Omi Chand had put all their lives at risk by his threat to reveal the plot to Siraj-ud-dowla that Clive could not forgive.

And yet, paradoxically, it was Clive alone who showed compassion when Omi Chand, half demented, came to him a few days later for help. He pointed out that the merchant was still exceedingly wealthy and suggested that a rest in the pagoda near Malda might soothe him.

Omi Chand agreed. But it seems not to have done him much good. Though Clive subsequently speaks of him dealing in saltpetre at Patna, the Marwari merchant never fully recovered from the shock of losing his expected fortune, and perhaps the worse shock of realising that he had been out-played at his own game by Clive and 'the Gentlemen of Bengal.'

There was a curious sequel to this denouement. Until then, Omi Chand had been mean and avaricious. He had always dressed as soberly as possible, and had never spent a penny more than was necessary. After that traumatic day he changed completely, as if by losing his prize-money he lost also his avarice. From then until his death eighteen months later, he dressed in extravagant clothes, with great jewels on his fingers and hanging from his neck. People who saw him thought this a sign of insanity, but perhaps it was sanity at last.

Another victim was to suffer a worse fate. Siraj-ud-dowla in his flight up-river had, after four days, reached Rajmahal, ninety miles from Moorshedabad.

The rowers were exhausted. Siraj-ud-dowla's boat pulled into the bank. The ex-Nawab went ashore, and strolled into what appeared to be a deserted garden.

But there was a man there who recognised him, a fakir who was unlikely ever to forget the prince. Thirteen months earlier, in a fit of petulant rage, Siraj-ud-dowla had had both the fakir's ears cut off.

The fakir went straight to Mir Jaffar's brother who lived at Rajmahal, and told of the arrival of the fugitive prince.

Siraj-ud-dowla was arrested and taken back to Moorshedabad.

Frantic now with fear, he begged Mir Jaffar to spare him. The new Nawab seemed touched with pity, but his son Miran, backed by a number of other advisors, warned that if he let the wretched man live he would merely be the centre for further possible rebellions.

Mir Jaffar had little or no understanding of politics let alone statesmanship. Harassed and uncertain, he handed Siraj-ud-dowla over to Miran.

That night, Miran had Siraj-ud-dowla beheaded.

Mir Jaffar, knowing that Clive had advocated mercy where the ex-Nawab was concerned, hurried round the next day to 'explain' the necessity of having put the Nawab to death. It was, he explained, purely 'political'. Mir Jaffar had

9   Aliverdi Khan (centre) with his grandson and successor, Siraj-ud-dowla (extreme right). The
size of the characters has nothing to do with their physical appearance, but are tokens of their
importance. The larger the figure, the more important he is. *(Victoria & Albert Museum. Crown
Copyright)*

10 The ruler of Bengal, Aliverdi Khan, out hunting. Indian princes usually had at
the Court a number of fine artists to record the main events that took place.
Aliverdi's grandson, the unfortunate Siraj-ud-dowla, thought they were useless
and got rid of them all when he became ruler. *(Victoria & Albert Museum. Crown
Copyright)*

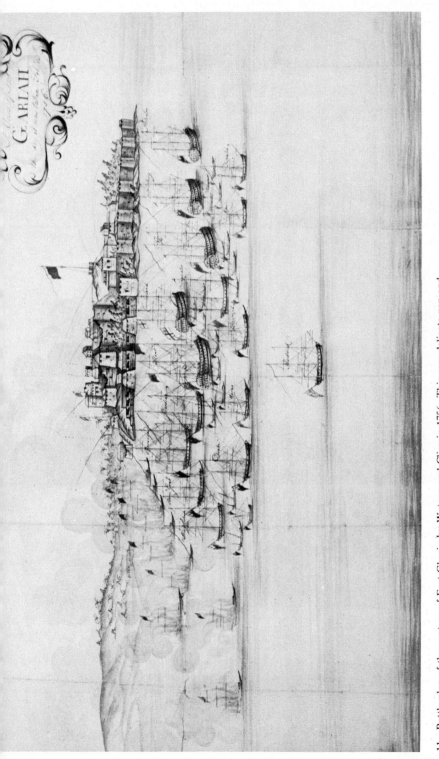

11　Battle plan of the capture of Fort Gheria by Watson and Clive in 1756. This very delicate pen-and-wash sketch was done on board one of the ships the day after the attack. (*India Records Office*)

12 A dramatised reconstruction of the scene in the Black Hole of Calcutta. When news of
the terrible disaster reached England, all kinds of 'artistic' impressions appeared.
They continued to do so for over a century after the event. *(Radio Times Hulton Picture
Library)*

definite information that Law and his French army had been within three hours' march of Siraj-ud-dowla when he was at Rajmahal. If the ex-Nawab were still alive, Law would have continued his march on Moorshedabad.

Whether Clive believed this story or not is not revealed. In his own report, he merely states: 'Next morning the Nabob [Nawab] paid me a visit, and thought it necessary to palliate the matter on motives of policy. . . .'

At all events, he sent Eyre Coote at the head of a detachment of troops chasing after Law, but Law, by forced marches, retraced his steps to Patna. Once outside Bengal, he was safe. Coote's sepoys refused to cross the frontier, and Eyre Coote returned to Clive, waiting somewhat impatiently at Moorshedabad.

Clive had his own worries. The usual wrangles broke out between the Army and the Navy on how the prize-money was to be shared out. Clive's handling of these quarrels, and, in particular his insistence that the Navy should be treated as generously as the Army, brought a growl of appreciation from Watson. His confidential aide-de-camp reported to Clive that the grateful Admiral drank every day 'a bumper' to his health.

Alas, he was not destined to drink these bumpers for long. On 12 August the Admiral contracted a 'putrid' fever. He died on 16 August.

Drake, the re-instated Governor, and the newly re-appointed committee at Calcutta were also behaving in a very fractious way. They were happy to let Clive win victories for them, but did not much relish the idea of having such a martinet in charge of the Council. Clive on his part never concealed his contempt for these cowardly and rapacious 'Gentlemen of Bengal'.

There was George Pigot and the Madras Council.

Faced with growing threats to Madras, Pigot, Stringer Lawrence and the other Directors were almost begging Clive to return. He was the only man, they felt, who could successfully save Madras from the French.

Clive was in an awkward position. His affection for his real friends in Madras was genuine. Though he felt that Stringer Lawrence, despite Aldercron's 'help', would be match enough for Lally, he could understand their anxiety. At the same time he wasn't at all happy at leaving Mir Jaffar alone to face the difficult business of ruling Bengal.

Mir Jaffar was a soldier. He owed his promotion to Siraj-ud-dowla's grandfather, a fact that makes his treacherous behaviour towards the grandson even less forgivable. He had commanded the late Nawab's army when it marched on Fort William. It was troops under his command who had imprisoned Holwell and the rest in 'the Black Hole'. He was faced with a bankrupt treasury and there was distinct possibility that Law would persuade the Nawab of Oudh, with whom he had taken refuge, to attack him.

Clive returned to Calcutta as soon as Eyre Coote arrived back from his hopeless chase of Law. He arrived in time to take part in Watson's funeral. Despite their earlier quarrels, Clive was genuinely sorry to see the cantankerous old seaman go. He was able, in a letter to the Directors, to speak of Watson's 'generosity, disinterestedness and zeal for service'. They had fought together both against the enemy and between themselves. He would miss him. Sir George Pocock took over command of the squadron.

Clive was now a very wealthy man. Everybody who took part in the battle of Plassey received his cut. Even the most junior ensign got £3,000. Clive, as commander-in-chief, received £20,000. He collected another £28,000 as a member of the Council, the other members receiving £24,000 each. Mir Jaffar, in a burst of gratitude, gave him the huge sum of £160,000. In one way and another he had £243,000 (equivalent to £2,500,000 today). Four years earlier he had returned to England with the moderate fortune of £40,000. Now he was nearly six times wealthier.

As before, his family's interests were his first concern. Margaret was with him and happily shared his dangers and difficulties. His thoughts were for those in England.

He wrote to his agents telling them to pay £2,000 to each of his five sisters, Rebecca, Sarah, Judith, Frances and Anne.

In his letter to his father, written shortly after Plassey, announcing this, he added: 'I would advise the lasses to marry as soon as possible, for they have no time to lose.'

He also made arrangements to pay his father an annuity of £500, so that the old man could stop the unprofitable business of practising the Law. He allocated £300 for the purchase and maintenance of a coach for his parents.

Clive senior's gratitude and pride was boundless. Gone for ever were even the memories of his earlier criticisms. In a letter to his son commenting on these arrangements, he wrote: 'The whole country is in transports for the glory and success their countryman has gained. Come away and let us rejoice together!'

But later a certain unease entered his correspondence when he had to admit that because of the death of a man for whom he stood surety, he owed £9,000 to the Treasury. The Duke of Newcastle had given him time to pay. He felt that he owed his son more than enough already. However, optimism soon broke out.

'Thank God,' he wrote, 'you have so much power!'

Another person who was giving him trouble was his old friend Edmund Maskelyne, Margaret's brother. Edmund had not done at all well after he had joined the Army. There had been some bother over his behaviour whilst, as a Captain, he had for a while in 1757 been in command of the fort at Arcot that Clive had defended so brilliantly. He had refused to carry out orders.

Clive decided that it would be best for all concerned if his old friend and brother-in-law were sent back to England.

He gave Edmund £10,000 and a letter of introduction to Clive senior. In it, Clive writes hopefully: 'I beg you will assist in settling him in the world, and in getting him a good wife.'

Margaret also received letters written in long careful

handwriting on sheets that folded up to form their own envelopes. Sarah Clive, a cousin, wrote to Margaret about '. . . the Eastern Prince the Colonel [as the younger members of his family called Clive] is so good as to say he will get for me. I can't possibly refuse him. I have a taste to be a princess.'

However, she adds prudently: 'As for Captain Clack, you are so good to think of for me, if this Prince don't care to take so long a voyage, don't leave the Captain behind. The war makes men very scarce.'

The letter ends with the wish that 'the Colonel and all his family may be in a ship, the sails filled with most prosperous gales, that will, soon as possible, send you safe to your own country and friends. . . .'

It was Robert and Margaret Clive's greatest wish too.

Chapter 14

Governor of Bengal

It was not so easy to get away.

As the days went by, Mir Jaffar showed that, without Clive's support, he would not last long as Nawab. In order to pay off the huge debts owing to the East India Company and other claimants, he resorted to the old 'soak the rich' policy, in this case the very Marwari bankers who had put him in power. They soon began to plot against him, just as they had previously plotted against Siraj-ud-dowla.

'The Gentlemen of Bengal' somewhat reluctantly asked Clive to be President, and soon the Directors in Leadenhall Street itself, under the chairmanship of Payne, got rid of Drake completely, and appointed Clive Governor of Bengal.

This was the first time that an employee of the East India Company had held such a position. Not only was he in charge of the Company's affairs for the whole province, including the administration of the 900 square miles given to the Company, but he was, in fact, the true ruler of Bengal. As Mir Jaffar became more and more dependent on Clive, so Clive's power increased. And as it did so, he began to see beyond the commercial requirement of a private company based on the City of London. He began to look at Bengal as Dupleix had looked at the Carnatic: the power base from which British influence, as opposed to Company influence, could operate.

In the meantime, although the Madras Council needed every English soldier it could get, it managed, by the end of 1757, to get rid of the embarassing Aldercron; but only at the cost of losing the 39th Foot. Aldercron took it with him. All the same, several officers and 350 men transferred to the

Company. Stringer Lawrence took over command once again.

By the end of April 1758 Lally waiting at Pondicherry, had twelve hundred fresh troops and plenty of guns. He was supported by a powerful French fleet commanded by d'Ache. He had full power over all the French troops in India, and had instructions from the French Government to push the English out of India once and for all.

He was a bold, somewhat over-bearing man, and set out immediately to achieve his objective. Within five weeks indeed he had captured Fort St David and with it the town of Cuddalore.

Clive was furious and ashamed at what he considered to be the feeble defence put up by the defenders of the fort. He had a special feeling for Fort St David. It had been the place where he had first learnt the business of war. It had seen his first Governorship. Now it had fallen. Sarcastically he wrote to Pigot at Madras: 'Were our enemies supplied with wings, that they could fly into the place?'

By December, Lally had occupied Madras town as well and laid siege to Fort St George.

Despite Pigot's pleas, Clive remained in Bengal. Mir Jaffar became increasingly irritable whenever it seemed that Clive was about to leave him. Scrafton, who had now taken Watts's place at Moorshedabad, never ceased to report the nervousness of the new Nawab. Mir Jaffar was beginning to see that becoming the ruler of the Bengal was not as wonderful a matter as he had first thought. He began to hate the East India Company officials. The only one he liked and trusted was Clive. Miran had already tried to raise a rebellion against the Company and was furious when Clive reinstated the Marwari merchants.

Clive was quite convinced that Stringer Lawrence could hold Madras. Lawrence had what was for India, where tiny European armies operated with enormous effect, quite a considerable force: 1,600 Europeans, including 900 men from Colonel Draper's regiment, the 79th just arrived from

England as well as 2,220 sepoys and 153 mixed troops. A detachment of 140 Royal Artillery men gave power to his guns.

D'Ache, the French admiral, remembering perhaps the fate of La Bourdonnais, had always been unwilling to support Lally in his plans for the capture of Madras. After being defeated by Pocock off Tranquebar, he prudently withdrew most of his ships from the coast. He did, however, render Lally one service before going: he captured a Dutch ship, though France and Holland were officially at peace. There was enough cash on board the captured ship for Lally to keep going for quite a while.

To Clive, watching these events from Bengal, it seemed that he could help Pigot and Stringer Lawrence best by attacking de Bussy in the Northern Circars, the coast-line joining the Coromandel Coast with Bengal. In doing this he would draw off French troops from the siege of Madras, besides capturing large tracts of country previously under French control. An English officer Colonel Forde, who had previously served with the 39th Foot but had remained in India after Aldercron had gone home, was in command. Kilpatrick was dead, and Coote was too junior.

Clive was, as usual, explicit and direct in his views. In a letter to Pigot he wrote: 'From the several accounts I have received of M Lally, I do not entertain the high opinion of him which he seems to have gained upon the coast; and, indeed, his late behaviour has confirmed me in this opinion. Captain Monchanin, who is here, received a letter from his brother at Paris, informing him of the manner in which these troops were raised: they are not draughted out of any of the regiments of France, but are composed of foreigners and deserters; these latter had a pardon promised them on condition of enlisting for the East Indies.'

So Clive allowed the siege of Madras to continue. His confidence was fully justified. The fort held out against Lally. On 30 January 1759 the *Shaftesbury,* an East India-man, broke through the few blockading French ships Lally had managed to retain. It was full of treasure and stores. The morale was good. There were detached English and Indian forces conducting harassing operations on the French lines of communication. Joseph Smith held Trichinopoly with so small a garrison that the French prisoners, left over from the unofficial war that had been concluded five years earlier, outnumbered him by five to one.

By the middle of February 1759, Lally was poised for the final assault on Fort St George. But on 16 February, Pocock's squadron appeared off Madras, a few hours before the intended assault was to start. It was enough for Lally. It was already doubtful whether he had sufficiently well-trained troops to carry the fort. The appearance of the Navy decided the issue. He broke off the siege and retreated to Pondicherry leaving behind, in the abandoned French trenches, fifty-two guns.

Warren Hastings, in the meantime, then aged twenty-five, had replaced Scrafton at Moorshedabad. Although relationships between Clive and Warren Hastings were not too good, the latter kept Clive always punctiliously aware of what was happening at that sumptuous, though shaky court.

The new threat came from Delhi itself. Shah Zada, or Shah Alam, as he is more usually called, was the Mogul Emperor's eldest son. Wishing to emulate Nizam-ul-Mulk who in 1724, more than thirty years earlier, had left Delhi to found Hyderabad, Shah Alam also decided to become the head of one of the Emperor's Component States.

He chose Bengal where he knew disaffection was increasing against Mir Jaffar. Collecting together a band of adventurers and forty thousand men, he set off eastwards.

He was young and ambitious; but had a certain cunning. As he marched east, he called upon rulers of the provinces he entered to support him against Mir Jaffar. They were, after all, technically subjects of the Mogul and owed him allegiance. Some, such as the Nawab of Oudh, still sheltering Law and his Frenchmen, responded.

By an act of probably unconscious irony, Shah Alam also

called upon Clive to support his claim to Mir Jaffar's throne. After Plassey, Clive had been, like Dupleix before him, made a Mogul Prince. He had the rank of commander of 'Five thousand horse and six thousand Foot'. He was, theoretically at least, obliged to obey the instructions of the Mogul.

But, keeping strictly to the intricate rules of intrigue and counter-intrigue, at which he was now such a master, he replied that he had received no direct orders from the Mogul, and that he was anyhow 'under the strictest engagement with the present governor of the province to assist him at all times.'

Warren Hastings reported that Mir Jaffar was almost mad with worry; and the Nawab himself wrote every day begging Clive to come to his rescue.

Once his mind was made up, Clive acted with his usual decisive speed. There were very few troops left in Calcutta. All that could be spared had been sent to Madras or accompanied Colonel Forde on his expedition into the Northern Circars.

Leaving only the sick and wounded as a token force to defend Fort William, he collected 450 European troops and 2,500 sepoys and set off inland in order to confront Shah Alam's 40,000 men. He stopped long enough in Moorshedabad to prevent Mir Jaffar's troops, who had not been paid for some time, from mutinying; and then marched on towards Patna, which the ever growing rebel army was approaching.

He covered four hundred miles in twenty-three days, and such was the personal power of his name that wherever he went the rebel leaders immediately abandoned Shah Alam. Even Shah Alam's own personal troops simply disappeared as soon as it was known that Clive was approaching. The 40,000 vanished without a fight.

In the end, Shah Alam himself begged Clive to help him escape now from the opposition of his erstwhile allies and the fury of the Mogul in Delhi.

Clive sent him £1,000 and advised him to keep out of the way. Shah Alam took the money and the hint. The external danger was, at least for a time being, at an end.

Clive returned to Moorshedabad to find Mir Jaffar even more grateful than ever. The Nawab's first solution to Shah Alam's threat had been to offer the young man money. Clive had advised against this saying that it would only encourage others to attack.

Mir Jaffar, in his relief, gave Clive a jaghire or quit-rent with £30,000 a year. It was, in fact, the money that the East India Company paid for the rent of the land situated south of Calcutta. Mir Jaffar merely handed it all over to Clive.

It might now be thought that Clive could at last get back to England. Although he commanded regular troops he was not a regular officer. He was still a servant of the East India Company. There was nothing technically to prevent him returning home.

But a completely unexpected danger threatened him at a time when the climate was beginning to erode his strength again, and his military position was still weak.

The Dutch, on leaving India for Batavia, had kept a trading station at Chinsura on the Hooghli, north of Calcutta. The Dutch merchants had traded peacefully for many years, and had been careful to keep out of the squabbles of the French and the English, as well as the Indian princes around them.

Then suddenly, in October 1759, seven Dutch ships filled with Dutch and Malayan troops arrived at the mouth of the Hooghli from Batavia.

Warren Hastings had given Clive some warning of danger from this area, but had not been able to specify the exact details. It soon became evident, however, that Mir Jaffar, despite his assurances of eternal gratitude to Clive, had planned this coup with the Dutch. Indeed, his negotiations began in November 1758, before Clive set off against Shah Alam. They continued, although in a minor way, at the very time Mir Jaffar was clamouring for help, and were intensified after the collapse of Shah Alam's adventure.

The reason was jealousy. Mir Jaffar, encouraged by his

unreliable son, did not like the idea of having to rely so heavily on the English. The French influence was at an end in Bengal. There were no Indian rulers he could trust, or who were courageous enough to stand up to Clive. The Dutch, however, still had a reputation for military prowess. So Mir Jaffar discreetly approached the Dutch authorities at Chinsura.

They in turn informed Batavia. For some time, the Dutch had seen with envy the increasing wealth and influence of the East India Company in Bengal. They were eager to share in this wealth. At the same time, they were annoyed because Clive, as the businessman he could become at a moment's notice, had earlier got for the East India Company the monopoly of the saltpetre trade. Finally they were irked by the East India Company's insistence that only English pilots were to be employed on the Hooghli and that all vessels, including the Dutch, could be searched.

Clive was in a difficult position. He couldn't quite believe that his 'friend' Mir Jaffar, who owed him so much, and was so profuse in his thanks, could be quite so treacherous. But he was determined to find out.

He allowed Mir Jaffar to meet the Dutch fleet, ostensibly on a courtesy visit, and then got from Warren Hastings the evidence of Mir Jaffar's deceit.

So that was that.

But there were still other problems. England and Holland were at peace, although there was some speculation that war might break out between the two countries. Would, however, the English Government view the premature outbreak of hostilities between the two countries in India with pleasure? Might they not disown Clive altogether? Even bring him to trial?

Then there was a private consideration. As much as £180,000, the greater part of his newly acquired fortune was, at that very moment, passing through the hands of the Dutch in Batavia, on its way to England. As a member of the East India Company he could not send it through his own company.

Hardly a tactful moment to start a fight.

Clive, however, did not hesitate. He did not now want to see the establishment of another powerful European influence in Bengal which could, by its alliances with treacherous Nawabs like Mir Jaffar, threaten the East India Company.

Despite all the risks involved he decided to oppose the Dutch. He conscripted every European, Armenian and Eurasian he could find; strengthened the batteries that commanded the river, and placed heavy guns on the fort itself.

There were four English ships in the river at the time. Three of them were armed East Indiamen. He ordered these to move in close to Fort William, to act, if necessary, as mobile batteries. The fourth, and smallest, was sent out to sea to contact Admiral Cornish, who was cruising off the Arakan coast, with an urgent request to come to his help.

At this point Colonel Forde returned with his somewhat weary force from the Northern Circars. He had been completely successful in defeating the French (Lally had unwisely recalled the brilliant de Bussy) and thus both eliminated French influence at Hyderabad and contained a large force that might have been used in the siege of Madras.

Clive handed the military command over to Forde.

The Dutch sent what amounted to an ultimatum to the Council, and threatened reprisals if the movement of their warships up stream was opposed.

Clive, with his tongue somewhat in his cheek, replied that he was only carrying out Mir Jaffar's, and through him the Mogul's, orders, if he insisted on searching the Dutch ships for illegal arms and troops. As he pointed out, Mir Jaffar had entrusted to him before now the responsibility of keeping out unwanted disturbers of the peace and tranquillity of his country.

It was the tone of this letter as much as its contents that angered the Dutch. They immediately attacked and seized seven of the Company's grain-boats, and the little *Leopard Snow,* under command of Captain Barclay, sent out to contact Admiral Cornish. Guns and stores were transferred from the English to the Dutch ships. The English colours were publicly burnt.

At the same time, a party landed at Fulta and Riapore and burnt down the houses belonging to the Company's tenants.

Clive concluded that war had broken out in Europe between England and Holland, and that the Dutch had heard about it before him. It, at least, gave him an excuse to defend himself.

At the same time, he wrote immediately to Mir Jaffar, and informed him that as this was a European war he would not need his assistance. He added ironically that if the Nawab really wanted to show his sincerity and attachment for Clive, he could surround the Dutch settlements up-country and 'distress' them to the utmost.

Having thus neutralised his untrustworthy friend, he was free to deal with the Dutch.

He immediately sent Colonel Forde up-stream to capture any Dutch trading posts he encountered, and to prevent the Dutch from reaching their main station at Chinsura should they attempt to do so. Forde, although sick and officially out of service, set off on 19 November 1759 with the greater part of the small force of 370 European troops and 800 sepoys at Clive's disposal. . . .

Holwell, the survivor of the 'Black Hole of Calcutta' was put in charge of the scratch force of 300 militia and Portuguese left in Fort William.

Captain Wilson, in command of the three East Indiamen, was ordered to demand from the Dutch the immediate restitution of the captured ships, subjects and property. If the demand was not met he was immediately to 'sink, burn and destroy' the Dutch ships.

Wilson's three East Indiamen mounted 90 guns between them. The Dutch squadron consisted of four 36-gun ships, two of 26 guns and one of 16 guns. A total of 212 guns.

The Dutch admiral not unexpectedly refused to consider Clive's ultimatum. Wilson immediately attacked.

In little more than two hours, he had captured or sunk six

of the Dutch ships. The seventh made a dash down the river for the open sea, but was stopped at the mouth of the river by the *Oxford* and *Royal George* that had just arrived.

In the meantime, the Dutch land force, under command of a French soldier of fortune called Colonel Roussel, was marching, as Clive had anticipated, towards Chinsura. The force was a mixed one of 700 Europeans and 800 Malayans and a number of locally press-ganged troops.

Forde, somewhat doubtful of his international position and wishing to have his instructions in writing, asked Clive for the authorisation of an Order in Council.

Clive was playing whist when Forde's letter arrived.

Without rising from the table, he wrote on it: 'Dear Forde – Fight them immediately. I will send you the Order of Council tomorrow.'

Forde attacked. Within half an hour, the Dutch had lost 320 killed, 300, including Roussel himself, wounded and the rest captured.

In the meantime, Miran, Mir Jaffar's belligerent son, had moved to Chinsura with a force of six thousand cavalry. His objective had been to join up with the Dutch force when it arrived at Chinsura, and then turn on the English.

When, however, Miran heard that the Dutch had been routed, he did the usual volte-face, and decided to use his cavalry to eliminate what remained of the Dutch settlements in the area.

The Dutch, on suing for peace, also begged Clive to protect them from their erstwhile allies.

Clive moved in these negotiations with the same speed and determination as he had in the military sphere. He confronted Mir Jaffar – at one of the Nawab's more awkward meetings, one would imagine – and made him stop his truculent son from murdering all the Dutchmen he could find. He then imposed generous terms on the defeated Dutch. But he made a stipulation that the Dutch were never to maintain more than 125 European soldiers in Bengal, mainly as factory guards, and that they were to pay the cost and damage caused by the expedition.

Despite all this, his private fortune of £180,000, in transit with the Dutch East India, continued quietly on its way, and arrived safely, in due course, in London.

And, at last he and Margaret followed it a few months later, sailing from India on 25 February 1760 on board the *Royal George.*

'It appeared,' wrote one of his contemporaries, 'as if the soul was departing from the body of the Government of Bengal.'

As he sailed down the Hooghli he received a message from the Coromandel Coast telling him that Coote, now a Lieutenant-Colonel at the head of the 84th Regiment (later 2nd York and Lancaster) had decisively defeated the French at Wandiwash on 22 January. De Bussy had been captured, and Lally, wounded, had fled to Pondicherry.

It was the end of French power in India; for though Lally was to defend Pondicherry heroically for another eight months before surrendering, it was obvious to all that a French army would never again set out either to support a princely squabble or harass the East India Company.

The great dream of Dupleix, now living in poverty in Paris, was over.

Clive, at thirty-five, could look forward with an easy conscience to a future that must have seemed, from the deck of the *Royal George,* promisingly bright.

13a Admiral Watson, the Commander in charge of the British naval forces operating with Clive. Although cantankerous and taking offence easily, he was a loyal friend and had unusual streaks of generosity. It is said that he once tried to save the life of an Indian widow who was to be put 'ceremoniously' to death. *(National Maritime Museum)*

13b Eyre Coote who was appointed Governor of Fort William instead of Clive. Although the mix-up only lasted a day, and Eyre Coote fought with Clive at Plassey, they were never on friendly terms after this alleged 'snub'. *(National Army Museum)*

14 Eighteenth-century European house in India. Some were more magnificent than any house in the neighbourhood. Parties, European-style, would go on all night. Shaded walks would lead from one house to another, and then down to the river landing stage, so that however hot the weather, the guests did not have to walk in the sun. (*India Records Office*)

15 Naval operations in the capture of Chandernagore. This was a 'sea' versus land battle conducted in waters so narrow and infested with obstacles that the ships had hardly any room to manoeuvre at all. That they managed to break through the Chandernagore defences was a credit, Clive was quick to acknowledge, to Watson and his men. *(National Maritime Museum)*

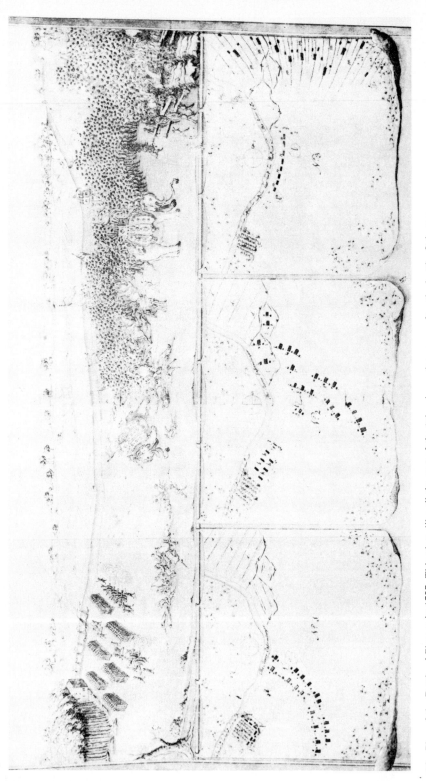

16　Plan of the Battle of Plassey in 1757. This plan, like all the rest of the 'plans' was drawn up after the battle. It is more a 'strip-cartoon' depiction of the main events of the battle than a working plan. Clive seized his opportunities as they occurred. (*India Records Office*)

Part Three

The Trembling Affluence of an Unsettled Fortune

Chapter 15

Eternal Return

Clive landed in England in the autumn of 1760. He was now a millionaire and perhaps the most famous man in England. He was the only real general, apart from Wolfe, that England had produced since Marlborough. Though the number of troops he commanded was always small, the effects of his victories were enormous. He had never lost a battle, and he had shown in the way that he handled the intricate negotiations with Mir Jaffar that he had an instinctive knowledge of statesmanship. His moderation in his handling of the Dutch showed that he could see beyond the immediate crisis.

He had been admired by George II. When the King had been asked, a few years earlier, whether a young peer might go as a volunteer to the Duke of Brunswick, he had replied: 'Pshaw! What can he learn there? If he wants to learn the art of war, let him go to Clive!'

And William Pitt in his speech on the Mutiny Bill had said: 'We had lost our glory, honour and reputation everywhere but in India. There the country had a heaven-born general who had never learnt the art of war. . . . Yet was he not afraid to attack a numerous army with a handful of men.'

Clive had, it would seem, every reason to hope for as magnificent a position in England as in Bengal.

But trouble started almost as soon as he got back: his health broke down. He had had an attack of rheumatism in 1759, but on the whole his health had been a little better the whole time he was in Bengal.

Now that he was safely back in his own country, reaction set in. His stomach, always delicate since his childhood illness, again gave him great pain. His liver had been functioning badly ever since 1752. He had taken drugs again. For a time he was so ill that it seemed that he might die.

Then there was the question of the recognition of his services by the Government. George II had died. George III was now on the throne. Although the King congratulated him on his achievements, he was slow in recognising them officially.

Clive had hoped for a British peerage. Instead, he had to be satisfied with an Irish peerage; and he had had to wait some time for that. He became eventually Lord Clive of Plassey in the Kingdom of Ireland.

In a letter written to a friend of his, Major Carnac, he recorded later: 'If health had not deserted me on my first arrival in England, in all probability I had been an English peer, instead of an Irish one, with the promise of a red riband.'

The trouble perhaps was that he was unwilling to put down the large sum of money that was customary in such cases, believing that his services to the country should have been enough. He continued his letter: 'I know I could have bought the title (which is usual), but that I was above; and the honours I have obtained are free and voluntary.'

He had turned in the meantime to the House of Commons, and in the elections of 1761 was elected member for Shrewsbury.

He was an admirer and follower of William Pitt. Pitt's grandfather, 'Diamond' Pitt, had also been in India, finishing as Governor of Fort St George in Madras. 'Diamond' Pitt was a tough violent man who had affection for only one member of what he called his 'unfortunate and cursed' family: William Pitt. The problems of the East India Company in India were thus familiar.

Pitt's mainspring was commerce. He had the backing of the City and he saw the struggle with France mainly as a commercial struggle. He was not concerned primarily with establishing an Empire, but in securing better trading conditions. As early as 1746 he had advocated an attack on

Canada, then under French control, mainly in order to secure the trade in fur and fish.

Pitt therefore watched Clive's progress in India with complete approval. Here was a young and able man, carrying out the very kind of commercial-cum-military warfare that Pitt approved of so heartily; and doing it, too, with the absolute minimum amount of men and money.

It was, oddly enough, Clive who was more 'progressive' than Pitt. Before leaving India he had written suggesting that the time had come for the British Government to take over the running of Indian affairs from the East India Company.

Pitt had acknowledged the letter and had thought the idea good; but he felt that the time had not yet come for such action.

Clive's career in Parliament was unusually muted. Perhaps he felt more at ease in the hot steamy intrigues of India than in the cooler atmosphere of the House of Commons. He was anyhow such a dedicated follower of Pitt's that when the latter resigned office in October 1761, Clive refused to serve under Pitt's successor, Lord Bute.

Bute had enormous personal influence over the young George III, and when he finally managed to bring Pitt down, he tried because of Pitt's popularity, to win over as many prominent men as he could; among them Clive. But Clive refused to consider the offers, tempting though they were. He remained a faithful supporter of Pitt and George Grenville, who on Pitt's retirement had resigned as Treasurer of the Navy.

He wrote to his friend Carnac on the subject: 'There is to be a most violent contest, at the meeting of Parliament, whether Bute or Newcastle is to govern this Kingdom; and the times are so critical that every member has an opportunity of fixing a price upon his services. I still continue to be one of those unfashionable kind of people who think very highly of independency. . . .'

He did, however, continue to keep close watch on foreign affairs, particularly where they affected India.

While his old rival, de Bussy, was carefully consulted when it came to preparing peace terms with the English, Clive was pointedly ignored by Bute.

Nevertheless he sent Bute a memorandum begging him to be careful to limit the number of men the French would be allowed to maintain on the Coromandel Coast, and not to allow any of them into Bengal, except as merchants.

Bute had the courtesy to acknowledge receipt of Clive's paper, and remarked that 'the lights you have thrown on the subject could not fail of being acceptable to me.'

In the treaty that was then drafted, these two points were included, but when it was signed in February 1763, thus bringing to an end the Seven Years' War as the long struggle came to be called, there were other conditions that Clive could not accept. Like Pitt, he deplored the fact that though the French had lost so much, they had yet been allowed to keep toe-holes in various parts of the world.

When it came to vote, he joined the minority who voted against the treaty, and thus placed himself outside the possibility of being granted office.

But he had another worry: it was the Court of Directors in London of the East India Company itself.

For some time, before leaving India, he had become discontented with the top-heavy and haphazard way the Company controlled, or failed to control, its Indian subsidiaries. Matters came to a head when an unnecessarily sharp and critical letter was received in Calcutta by the Council.

Immediately Clive, while still at Calcutta, and three other members of the Council, including Holwell, wrote an angry letter in reply. In it, they wrote: 'Permit us to say that the diction of your letter is most unworthy of yourselves and US, in whatever relation considered, either as masters to servants or gentlemen to gentlemen.'

The effect of this letter was to make the Court of Directors dismiss all four from future service with the Company.

So that when Clive arrived, in triumph, in London, he had

in fact been 'sacked' by the very people he had served so well.

However, for the sake of appearances, the East India Company Directors, at least in public, acclaimed, along with the rest of the country, Clive's great achievements.

But they were working against him behind his back. One of them was particularly anxious to harm Clive. That was the President of the Company itself, Sullivan.

Sullivan had at one time been a genuine admirer of Clive's.

But then friction had started over the Court's treatment of Forde, who had been dropped in favour of Coote. Sullivan had been enormously impressed by Coote during the latter's visit to England. He had ascribed Clive's preference for Forde to jealousy because Coote had been the young officer who had held Fort William on Admiral Watson's orders in defiance of Clive. He preferred Coote to Forde. As a result, Forde had never received, much to Clive's disgust, the recognition he deserved. Clive always stood by those he admired.

Sullivan had been infuriated by Clive's letter from Calcutta. But now there was a new reason for making life difficult for Clive. Sullivan was a friend of Bute, and Clive had contemptuously turned down all Bute's inducements to join his government.

Clive, seeing the danger, tried to take the presidency of the East India Company from Sullivan before trouble started and give it to a friend, but though he spent £100,000 in judicious bribery and was confident of victory, he was, for the first time in his life, defeated.

The victors lost no time in attacking him. And they chose to humiliate him over the jaghire he had received from Mir Jaffar in 1759. This was the quit-rent of £30,000 a year that the Company paid the Nawab of Bengal, in exchange for the right to collect rents in the area south of Calcutta. The sum of £100,000 was thus collected, giving the East India Company a nice profit of £70,000.

For the past four years, the Company's £30,000 had not been paid to the Nawab but to Clive's agents in Calcutta.

Now in 1763, orders were sent to Bengal that the £30,000 was no longer to be paid to Clive. In addition, accounts were to be sent immediately to London detailing exactly how much had been paid in this way to Clive.

The fight between Clive and Sullivan was on.

The situation was somewhat complicated and delicate. After Clive had left Bengal in 1760, Holwell had succeeded him for a while as Governor. Holwell, who had been shut up in the 'Black Hole' and seen so many of his friends die, hated Mir Jaffar; for Mir Jaffar had been the commander-in-chief of the army that was responsible for the tragedy.

Holwell immediately started to plot Mir Jaffar's downfall. Although these plans had not been carried out when the new Governor, Vansittart, was appointed, Holwell had no difficulty in persuading Vansittart to follow the same line.

The appointment, after a strong recommendation from Clive, was a curious one. Vansittart was an amiable, but not a determined man and was easily swayed. There were two much stronger claimants: Watts and Warren Hastings. Watts was considered not available, and Clive had little confidence in Warren Hastings.

Perhaps the apparent muddle when Warren Hastings was at Moorshedabad was behind this; or perhaps Clive, so sure in everything else, lacked the power to see his own strength reflected in others. He saw nothing remarkable in either Coote or Warren Hastings, yet after himself and Watts, they were the most able men in Bengal at the time.

However, Vansittart it was.

Encouraged by Holwell, it did not take him long to depose Mir Jaffar, whose violent son Miran had been killed by lightning on 2 July 1760. The heir apparent was then Mir Jaffar's own son-in-law Kasim Ali Khan.

The way it was done was simple. Vansittart, with or without reason, considered that Mir Jaffar was behind-hand with his payments to the Company.

162

So Vansittart called on Mir Jaffar at Moorshedabad. He took the precaution of bringing with him Caillard, now a colonel, and 180 European troops, 600 sepoys and four pieces of cannon.

Either Mir Jaffar would agree to Vansittart's new and exorbitant demands or the palace would be stormed.

Instead, Mir Jaffar offered to resign in favour of his son-in-law. In exchange he asked for safe conduct for himself and his family to Calcutta. The death of his son, the weariness of holding an office for which he was not suited, and a feeling of personal bitterness brought on this mood of depression.

His resignation was immediately accepted.

Although he himself had been raised to power through treachery, he showed a certain nobility in his retirement speech: 'The English', he said, 'placed me on the Musnud [throne]; you may depose me if you please.'

He pointed out that had he wished to do so, he could have raised twenty thousand men, and fought Vansittart, but he had not wished to fight those to whom he owed so much. 'Send me,' he begged, 'to Sabut Jung [Clive] for he will do me justice.'

But Clive was in England now, and would be for the next three years. Bengal was in the hands of the weak and inefficient Vansittart. There was no 'Daring in War' to inspire men to extend themselves.

So Mir Jaffar was packed off to exile, but did not disappear from the scene. As soon as he was safely out of Moorshedabad, he began to think about the ways and means of getting back again. In that hot steaming world of intrigue and plot, everything was possible. . . .

In the meantime, Vansittart and the Select Committee were in a euphoria of delight. Apart from the satisfaction of revenge, there was the usual installation bribe, this time £200,000, the new Nawab, Kasim Ali, had to find. It was carefully divided out amongst the members of the Select Committee, Vansittart keeping the largest share – £28,000 –

for himself.

So now, when Sullivan and his co-Directors in London were trying to stop Clive getting his yearly £30,000, they argued that even if Mir Jaffar had the right to grant the jaghire, which they did not admit, he lost that right when the Company deposed the Nawab.

These and other tortuous legal spin-abouts formed the basis of the Directors' case. Legal opinion, as usual, was divided. The Directors, however, confident that they could win on a technicality, pressed their case.

Clive brought a suit in Chancery against them, and informed the Governor of Bengal that if the Company there withheld the annual payment, he would sue in Calcutta as well.

Both sides now waited the outcome of the court case.

But events in Bengal were suddenly to play a decisive role.

The select Committee in Calcutta had, with its usual greed, arranged a grossly unfair system of inland transit duties. Goods accompanied with East India Company passes travelled free. All others paid a heavy tax.

Kasim Ali complained that, apart from the unfairness of the system, it was open to abuse. Genuine East India Company passes were sold at high prices. Faked passes were commonplace.

Vansittart, though weak, saw the injustice of this. He and Warren Hastings did what they could to change the system.

The Select Committee, the main beneficiaries of the lop-sided arrangement, were naturally not very keen even to bring the matter up for discussion, let alone make a decision against their interests.

However, Vansittart and Warren Hastings persevered. Some kind of compromise was eventually worked out. Company goods were to pay a flat rate duty of 9 per cent, all others 25 per cent. But even this very advantageous arrangement was turned down by the majority of the Council. Except where the salt trade was concerned, where 20 per cent was paid, all East India Company trade should carry no tax whatsoever.

Kasim Ali was very different from the shifty general who had preceded him. He was cool, clear-headed and strong. He had accepted Vansittart's compromise agreement, realising perhaps that this was at least a step in the right direction. When he learnt that the Select Committee, although it had given Vansittart full powers, now rejected the agreement, he immediately declared Bengal a free-trade area and abolished all duties.

Knowing that any action of this kind would bring the East India Company troops after him, he had prudently moved the seat of Government from Moorshedabad to Mungur, 320 miles from Calcutta. He had also raised a large army of 15,000 cavalry and 25,000 infantry. Remembering what had happened at Plassey, he was careful to train them on East India Company lines. He built an arms factory that turned out a first-class type of musket. He made a foundry for casting cannon. He trained a corps of artillerymen.

He had a good head for business and had put the affairs of his country onto a sound financial footing. Had Vansittart been able, or strong enough, to overrule his greedy Council, there can be little doubt that the new Nawab and the Company could have come to a satisfactory working agreement.

As it was, Ellis, a violent and pig-headed member of the Council, in charge of the Patna trading station, seized the town itself.

Kasim Ali sent his newly trained troops to retake the place. It was captured immediately.

Ellis attempting to escape, was captured and brought back to Patna. Amyatt, a personal friend of Clive's. and sent by the Select Committee to negotiate with Kasim Ali, was also taken, and killed while attempting to escape.

The Select Council immediately declared war on Kasim Ali and sent Major Adams of the 39th Foot, trained by Clive, after him. Adams fought three battles with Kasim Ali's troops. So well had Kasim Ali's men imbibed the Company's training that the battles of Katwa and Andhwa Nala were largely undecisive. But Adams' skill and the work of an English double-agent brought victory at the third battle: at Gheriah.

Kasim Ali fled to Oudh. But before leaving he ordered the massacre of 150 European prisoners, including Ellis, held at Patna.

The events at Patna had a decisive affect on the Court of Directors in London. In their panic they turned to Clive and asked him to go out to India again, to bring order back to Bengal, above all to stop the idiotic Directors out there doing what the French had failed to do: ruin the East India Company. They promised that the awkward matter of stopping Clive's jaghire would be dropped. He need have no more worry as far as that was concerned.

But Clive did not trust the London Directors any more than the 'Gentleman of Bengal.' There was no telling what Sullivan would do once Clive was safely out of the country.

With his customary bluntness, he refused to do anything until the Court of Directors had got rid of Sullivan as Chairman. He did not care who took his place, but he would not serve in any capacity under Sullivan. What, he asked, was the point of doing so, since his measures would be thwarted by a Chairman, who was not only ignorant of East India affairs but was his inveterate enemy?

Sullivan tried in every way to sway the Court against Clive, but there was nothing he could do. However, owing to the complex structure of the Company he could not be evicted from the Chairmanship.

In the meantime, every ship from Bengal brought further news of mismanagement, fraud and oppression. Something had to be done.

Clive was appointed Governor and Commander-in-Chief in March 1764.

The Directors, backed by Sullivan, immediately booked a passage for him on the first ship sailing for India. The reason for their haste was quite simple: there were to be General Court elections on 25 April next. With Clive out of the country, Sullivan's chances of re-election were brighter.

But Clive merely replied that he would not sail until the elections had been held. Sullivan tried to get Clive's appointment to Bengal cancelled; but this move also failed. There was nothing for it but tó face the elections.

It was an extremely passionate and hot-headed affair. When the votes were finally counted, 12 Directors had voted for Sullivan and 12 against. The deciding vote lay with the Deputy Chairman, a friend of Clive's. Rous, a supporter of Clive, now became Chairman. Bolton, another of Clive's party, became Deputy Chairman.

Despite his liver complaint, his gallstones, and the harsh struggle with Sullivan, Clive's private and personal life continued to be happy. Margaret had not only beauty, charm and wit but a deep resourceful store of strength. Her married life had not been moulded to a normal standard. She had had to face danger, disease, illness and dirt while she had travelled with Robert. She had had to leave her two young children, one of them dying, when they had left for India the last time in 1755. Now, this time, she had to stay at home as she was once again pregnant, and was in no condition to travel.

They had a fine house in London, and property in the country. Though they entertained, it was not on the same wild scale as after his first return. He was thirty-nine, but he was much older both physically and mentally. As a member of Parliament, and a recognised authority on Indian affairs, he tended to invite the political rather than the fashionable crowd. He was enormously fond of whist. Whist parties formed the excuse for many an evening-long session, when pipes would be smoked, port (when his gout, from which he also suffered from time to time, allowed) drunk, and the latest parliamentary gossip recounted.

He had a large family and many dependents. His income was estimated at £45,000 (£450,000 today), but he was enormously generous. Besides providing for his father, paying off the old man's debts, showering dowries upon his sisters, he kept alive a multitude of uncles and aunts. He put up £2,000 for his wife's cousin John Walsh's candidature as an M.P. Then there were his friends, foremost among them Stringer Lawrence, to whom he paid an annuity of £500 a year. Many others benefitted from his generosity. Once he entered the family circle he became the family man, and left at the door the mantle of statesman, general and astute businessman which was the sight most people saw of him.

So now, on 4 June 1764 he sailed once again for India. This time he was not alone as on the first occasion, nor with his wife as on the second, but with a fairly extensive staff. Besides two East India Company members, Sykes and Sumner, there were two Colonels newly appointed to East India Company brigades: Richard Smith and Sir Robert Barker. There was Ingham, his personal doctor, Henry Strachey, his private secretary, and Margaret's brother, Edmund.

Before sailing, he wrote to Margaret: 'My dearest wife,

'God only knows how much I have suffer'd in my Separation from the best of women, however the necessity of the thing and your good Sense will I am persuaded operate in the same Manner upon You as it has upon me, let us look forward towards the happy day of our Meeting which I think cannot be father distant than two Years, the education of our children will be pleasing Amusement & the busy Scene in which I shall be emply'd without embarking in any more military undertakings will greatly shorten our time of Absence.

'We shall be on board the *Kent* in two or three Hours and sa. immediately the wind being fair. You may be assur'd of hearing from me by the first opportunity which I believe will be from the Cape.'

But it wasn't to be. Clive had his usual bad luck where sailing was concerned. They were still only at Rio de Janeiro when they should have been at the Cape of Good Hope. The 'fair wind' out of Portsmouth had not been maintained, and the *Kent* was a slow lumbering ship. They reached Rio de Janeiro on 7 October, more than four months after leaving England. There were ships in the harbour that had left England a month after the *Kent* had sailed. One of these carried a letter from his wife. In answer to her letter, he wrote: 'Never entertain the least doubt of our meeting again' and promised that come what may 'nothing shall induce me to stay in Bengal beyond the Year 1765.'

In the meantime, events were on the move again in India.

After the Patna masscre and Kasim Ali's flight to Oudh, old Mir Jaffar was put back on the throne of Bengal. Once again he had to pay out vast sums of money from the depleted treasury. He had to agree to reimpose the hated transit tax, while allowing East India Company's goods tax-free movement. He even had to pay for the cost of the war the Calcutta Council had arbitrarily declared on Kasim Ali.

The country was now in an even worse state than before. The East India Company's monopoly was supreme. The abuses of the greedy members endless. The whole of Bengal was, in fact, being plundered by a few unscrupulous and merciless men. No consideration for the people of the country or even thought for the future held them back. Bengal was, to them, an Aladdin's chest full of gold and jewels to be endlessly scooped up.

Shah Alam, who a few years earlier had unsuccessfully threatened Mir Jaffar, was now Emperor at Delhi. He collected together a large well-trained army and set off eastwards once again. His objective was the same as before: depose Mir Jaffar and take over Bengal.

On the way east, he collected the Nawab of Oudh and the deposed Kasim Ali, eager to regain the throne of Bengal from his father-in-law. Their combined strength was fifty thousand.

The East India Company raised 1,200 English troops and 3,000 sepoys, and placed the force under the command of Major Hector Munro. Despite a mutiny just before the battle and odds of ten to one, Munro succeeded at Buxar in defeating Shah Alam's army.

As a result, Kasim Ali fled westwards once again, the Nawab of Oudh submitted, and, most significant of all, Shah Alam abandoned his allies and joined the English.

The battle took place on 23 October 1764. Clive's ship was then at Rio de Janeiro waiting for a favourable wind to take him across the South Atlantic to Cape Town.

The long tedious journey, battling against winds and storms went on. It took him nearly six months to sail from Rio de Janeiro to Madras. He arrived there on 10 April 1765, only to learn that the old intriguer Mir Jaffar had died on 25 February.

His friend George Pigot had retired with a huge fortune of £400,000, gained mainly from lending money to hard-up Princes at a high interest rate. His intention was to buy a peerage and live as an English country gentleman. The Carnatic anyhow was quiet. After the signing of peace in 1763, all disruptive French activity was at an end. The 'English' Nawab was still on the throne; and Hyderabad no longer had a Frenchman in control.

So Clive sailed on, pondering the new problem that Mir Jaffar's death had produced. On top of all his other difficulties, there would be that of the succession.

The original successor, Mir Jaffar's son Miran who had died a few years before his father, also had a son, aged six. Clive decided, whilst sailing towards Calcutta, to recognise this boy as the ruler of Bengal.

On arriving in Calcutta, in May 1765, however, he found that, contrary to instructions, the Council of Directors had already recognised Nazim-ud-dowla, the eighteen-year-old younger son of Mir Jaffar, as Nawab. The reason for their action was quite simple: at eighteen, the new Nawab had the keys to the treasury, the young grandson had not. The Directors collected a further £139,357 as a result of this move.

Clive was furious.

He had long come to the conclusion that the dual system of control could never work properly. Either the Nawab should run the country as in the old days, or the East India Company should be in complete control. But it was impossible to go back to the old days. The only solution was to take over the whole country.

No Nawab of the future would accept a weak English trading company. His need for English soldiers to fend off his greedy neighbours would make this impossible. Equally no East India Company would be prepared to adopt a humble attitude towards the Nawab while he owed his position to English protection.

Dupleix had had a vision of French imperialism, but imperialism was thrust upon Englishmen of the eighteenth century. Even Pitt in his 'drive for Empire' saw it in terms of trade; and though Clive wanted the British Government to take over from the East India Company, it was because he felt that the Company just wasn't made to rule an area as large as Bengal.

Had Pitt remained in office, there was just a chance that this might have happened. With Pitt out of office, there was none.

As Clive saw it, there was nothing for it but to take over the whole of Bengal. He had hoped to do this by ruling by proxy through Mir Jaffar's six-year-old grandson.

By the time the grandson grew up, a new and better generation of Company officials might have been trained to take over as rulers. It wasn't the best solution; but it was better for the people of the country, the Nawab and the East India Company, than if the present chaotic state of affairs continued. Since revolutions were so profitable, they would always exist.

Clive's fury, therefore, on arriving at Calcutta to find that an unknown young man had been installed can be imagined. Suppose he were another Kasim Ali, tough strong and able? All Clive's plans would be destroyed.

However, he could not undo the work of the Calcutta

Directors even though Vansittart had now left. Spencer, the new President, was no better than his predecessor.

Nor could he, holding his views, engineer another revolution with all that it would cost.

He decided to see this new young Nawab and went to Moorshedabad. Clive immediately realised that the young man had neither the intellectual nor the moral qualities to rule for a single day.

He then quickly put the plan he had worked out to the Nawab. It was simply that the East India Company should be responsible for collecting and administering the revenue for the whole of Bengal.

The Nawab demanded, somewhat petulantly, what was there in it for him?

A yearly fixed income of £50,000 to pay for his personal and Court expenses.

The Nawab hesitated.

Clive raised the figure to £53,000.

The Nawab smiled.

'Thank God,' he said, 'I shall now be able to have as many dancing girls as I please.'

Chapter 16

Reform

In the meantime, Clive also acted against the Select Committee itself. He produced the new contracts that had been sent out earlier. These, he indicated, had to be signed, or else. . . . Since they deprived the Committee members of all their power to accept bribes and make huge fortunes, they were not exactly welcome. Some, like the overbearing George Johnstone, tried to bully Clive out of enforcing these decrees, just as they had done with Vansittart.

But Clive was not like Vansittart. He turned on Johnstone and asked him point blank whether he was challenging the Court's authority? Johnstone tried to bluff it out; but Clive remained cold and indifferent. In the end, Johnstone evaded the issue and mumbled that he had never had the least intention of doing such a thing.

'Upon which,' records Clive, not without a certain glee, 'there was an appearance of very long and pale countenances, and not one of the Council uttered another syllable.'

However the depth of the double-dealing, corruption and straight robbery which he found depressed him.

Despairingly, he wrote: 'Alas! how is the English name sunk!'

When he discovered that Spencer, Johnstone and Leycester and other Directors had read the instructions sent from London that no further sums were to be taken from Indian princes placed on the throne, and then had immediately approached Nazim-ud-dowla and sold the throne to him, he was so furious that he dismissed them all upon the spot.

Their anger against him increased. Had he not accepted huge sums of money from Mir Jaffar when he put him on the throne after Plassey? Were they doing anything different but playing the same game? Didn't everybody do it out here?

Clive retorted that the cases were quite different. There had been no prohibition on the acceptance of money from foreign princes at the time of Plassey. Now there was. Besides, he and those with him at Plassey believed that they were performing a public duty replacing the corrupt government of Siraj-ud-dowla by one they hoped would bring prosperity to everyone in Bengal.

In truth, the East India Company was not built to deal with the situation that had arisen. It was a trading company that operated in a risky and often dangerous environment. It needed adventurous men, who were prepared to risk anything – health, life, reputation – to gain huge fortunes. Now, suddenly, it was expected to play a political role in a country larger than England. It needed to produce administrators not adventurers. But administrators with strict codes of honour and honesty were just the people neither to be attracted to nor to be sought by the Company.

Clive was an exception. So were Watts and Warren Hastings. They were the only ones. For though they started as adventurers, they realised that the situation was changing, that the old piracy was doomed, that the era of the administrator was beginning.

It was all right getting the dancing-girl-mad Nawab to agree to a transfer of power, but it was also necessary to have this alteration recognised by neighbouring states and sanctioned by the Mogul himself.

Clive consequently called on the Nawab of'Oudh who happened to be on a visit to Benares. The Nawab, recently defeated by the East India Company troops at Buxar dreaded the visit. He was prepared for Clive to lay down excessive terms.

Instead, the Englishman was not only exceedingly generous but asked the Nawab to state his own requirements. In this way, the Nawab retained the whole of Oudh and various other concessions. He was only required to pay the, to him, negligible sum of £600,000 as compensation to the Company for the expense of the war. A defensive alliance between Oudh, Bengal and the Company was signed. The Nawab could, whenever he liked, hire East India Company troops for his own defence.

Armed now with the grateful support of the Nawab of Oudh, Clive went on to Allahabad where the Mogul Shah Alam was waiting.

The last time the two men had had any dealings was when Clive had given the young man £1,000 and told him to make himself scarce. Now, he was the Mogul himself, but since his defeat at Buxar, Shah Alam, his capital taken by the Mahrattas, had come over to the East India Company. He thus expected a great number of concessions in return for his recognition of the Company's right to administer the Bengali finances.

But Clive, who knew exactly how to negotiate with Shah Alam, became tough.

While he had treated the Nawab of Oudh with generosity and thus obtained his support, he knew that, despite his threats, Shah Alam was not in the least secure. The Mogul had hoped that Clive would supply him with troops in order to recapture Delhi, but Clive merely said that the Mogul should live in the area, and accept the generous rent the Company was prepared to pay for Shah Alam's recognition of the new *status quo.*

Clive had thus, within a few months of his arrival at Calcutta, settled four difficult problems. He had effectively deprived the Select Committee of their personal power. He had taken over Bengal. He got the Emperor's approval for doing so, and finally, by his 'soft' treatment of the Nawab of Oudh, he had secured peace in the area.

When he returned to India, he realised that, in his own words, 'tomorrow the whole Mogul power is in our grasp'. But unlike Dupleix, he mixed realism with perception. It was, perhaps, this more than anything else that has made his name known, even today, when conditions are so different. He was not an 'Empire Builder'. He was not a moraliser. He was a practical man, enormously courageous, who when faced with a problem, whatever it might be, saw immediately a possible solution; and went straight for it with single-minded determination.

Whether he was defending Arcot, winning Plassey or involved in the dirty backwash of politics or business, he brought an odd sense of integrity. Even his less honourable dealings seem to be touched by it. In theory, one should deplore the fact that he forged Admiral Watson's signature to the false treaty with Omi Chand, yet one is left with the feeling: he was right.

This 'rightness' emerges time after time. His assessment of the situation in India then was right. The East India Company, as it was then constituted, could not, even if it had wished to, control and administer such vast areas. It would have difficulty enough dealing with Bengal.

Let others have dreams of empires. Clive was content to consolidate what he had achieved. When this was done, there would be time to turn, in the future, to further expansion.

In the meantime, he was faced with an awkward problem. He had stopped the practice of allowing Company servants to make huge personal fortunes. But what was he to put in its place? Despite his suggestions the Court of Directors refused to increase the pay of their servants. While the old advantages had gone, the inadequate pay remained. It was impossible for the Company servants to live on their salaries. Only by supplementing it with private trade could they exist. But private trade was forbidden.

Clive's solution was the creation of a Society of Trade. It was a Government-run society. It worked on the principle that its profits were to be shared out among the employees according to their rank and position. It traded mainly in salt, betel-nut and tobacco.

Though it sounded serviceable enough in theory, it did not work out in fact. It created a monopoly, particularly in salt. The Company officials extorted from the population an exorbitant price. At the same time, the distribution of profits was also subject to abuse. The Society of Trade became hated by all concerned, and Clive's name suffered because of it. It ran for two years and was then abolished. It was one of Clive's few failures. He was never satisfactorily able to solve that particular problem.

On the other hand, he displayed an act of personal generosity that made up for some of his unpopularity. Mir Jaffar, in his will, had left Clive a personal bequest of £70,000. It was nothing to do with the Company. Clive could do as he liked with it. He allocated the whole amount to a trust, known as Clive's Fund. The proceeds were to be paid to retired East India Company members, merchants or soldiers who were in need.

But, generous though this action might be, it did not prevent growing discontent among the civil servants of the East India Company.

The trouble went back to the massacre at Patna, which Kasim Ali had ordered before fleeing to Oudh after his defeat by Adams. Among the 150 Europeans killed were a considerable number of the more senior members of the East India Company.

The loss had been made up by the promotion of many younger and much less experienced men. Clive was not at all happy at the slapdash way these younger men were behaving.

He decided to bring from Madras four experienced men, and place them above the recently promoted employees.

The latter reacted violently to this proposal. They announced that they would boycott the new arrivals and refuse to take orders. Clive considered the young men unfit to manage their own affairs even, 'to the extent', as he wrote in his letter to the Court of Directors in London on 31 January 1766, 'of forty shillings.'

The 'mutineers' then sent a list of grievances to the Court of Directors; but Clive merely carried on with his plans, and after a certain amount of grumbling the revolt collapsed and the young men accepted Clive's authority again. But it did not add to his popularity.

Hardly had he dealt with this attempted mutiny by the civilian side of the Company than he found himself facing a much more serious threat from the East India Company's own private army.

With the enormous expansion of the Company's position after Plassey and the struggle with France, the small unofficial armed forces that the Company kept for self-protection had been developed into a full-scale and carefully balanced force.

It now consisted of three brigades. Its overall command was in the hands of Clive's old friend Carnac, now a General. Although it was not officially part of the Regular Army, the Government allowed it to exist. If nothing else, it was an economic way of keeping a military force stationed in India. For the East India Company, not the Government, paid for its upkeep, paid its officers and men and supplied all the armaments, ammunition and transport it needed.

It consisted to a large extent of sepoy regiments, stiffened here and there with wholly European battalions. Gone were the days when the unreliable peons were enlisted. Both the Europeans and sepoys were professional soldiers, highly trained and extremely efficient.

The officers were all Europeans, and mainly English. Some had served in the Regular Army and then, in search of adventure or higher pay, or both, had transferred to the East India Company's units. It was from this basis that the Indian Army was one day to be formed. Even today, the present Indian Army owes its general structure to that early experimental period when Clive and his commanders were building up their force.

Clive's dual capacity of being both a Commander-in-Chief and an Administrator was evident throughout his life in India. At each stage, whether as a young Captain or an experienced Governor, he always appeared in one role or another. Sometimes in both.

Although, as he promised Margaret before leaving London, he would not take an active military role whilst in India this time, he was very much still the Supreme Commander. So that when the threatened mutiny of his own army seemed inevitable, it was to him the loyal elements turned for a solution.

The trouble arose over the question of the double batta.

The batta was a form of field allowance the Company's officers drew when away from their base or home station.

After Plassey, at Clive's own insistence, Mir Jaffar gave all officers receiving a batta, an equal sum from his own treasury. This was known as the double batta.

For some time now, the Court of Directors in London had issued instructions that the double batta was to cease. But neither Vansittart nor Spencer had dared to put the ban into effect.

It remained for Clive to do so.

In September 1765, he announced that the double batta would cease as from 1 January 1766; except for the Second Brigade, under Colonel Richard Smith, stationed at Allahabad. It had been sent there at the request of Shah Alam to stop the Mahrattas from pursuing him. The double batta for the Second Brigade would only continue as long as the brigade was in the field. It would cease as soon as it returned to its base.

For the other two brigades, the First under the command of Lieutenant-Colonel Sir R. Fletcher at Monghyr, and the Third commanded by Colonel Sir Robert Barker at Bangipore the order was to come into effect as planned on 1 January 1766. This duly occurred.

It seemed at first as if the officers, although grumbling at the measures, had accepted them. But in fact, this was not the case at all. Secret meetings were held in each of the brigades and all officers were asked to resign their commissions on the first of June, unless the double batta were restored.

In order to avoid a charge of mutiny they were to refuse the usual advance of pay for June. They were to enter into a bond of £500 per head, not to accept a commission again, until the double batta had been restored; and in order to give Clive and the Council time to come to terms, they agreed to serve as volunteers until 15 June 1766.

It was a difficult moment.

Between 50,000 and 60,000 Mahrattas were marching on Corah, about 150 miles from Allahabad.

Colonel Smith's Second Brigade were ordered forward; but already a number of officers in it had signed the agreement. In all something like one hundred and thirty officers from the three brigades concerned had signed agreements.

Clive got to hear of the plot when he was visiting Moorshedabad on revenue business with his friend and Commander-in-Chief Carnac, in the middle of April. A letter signed 'Full Batta' was sent to Carnac asking him, of all people, to resign his commission and join the mutineers.

Carnac promptly showed Clive the letter.

The plot had anyhow been made public earlier during a squabble between two junior officers.

Because of this, the conspirators decided to put forward the resignation date to the first of May.

The Mahrattas were getting closer every day.

With the great majority of its officers on the point of walking out, the chances of the army holding together, let alone stopping the Mahrattas, was slim. It was this knowledge that encouraged the prospective mutineers to believe that the double batta would soon be restored.

Nobody seemed to know exactly who was behind the 'Full Batta' threats, nor whether the brigade commanders themselves were implicated. Perhaps all the Company troops were in league with their officers. There might be a full-scale mutiny at any minute.

The temptation to restore the double batta was very great. Without the Army, Clive was powerless. It seemed a small enough concession to secure the loyalty of his own forces. And, after all, the Company could do what it liked with its own troops.

But Clive knew that if he gave way, the Army realising its power, would become paramount. Other dissatisfactions would be sure to arise in the future. If the Army knew that it only had to threaten mutiny to get what it wanted, it would not be long before the military and not the civil side of the East India Company commanded in Bengal.

Clive acted with his usual decisiveness.

On 29 April, he sent an express message to the Council at Calcutta warning them of what was about to happen. He instructed them to write immediately to Madras calling all officers and cadets who could be spared to stand by for immediate trans-shipment to Bengal. He told the Council to warn Madras of the approach of the Mahrattas and to give the number of dissident officers. Finally, he informed the Council that they were never, under any circumstances, to employ any of the one hundred and thirty officers.

It was a time to stand firm for, he observed, 'such a spirit must at all hazards be suppressed at the birth, unless we determine upon seeing the government of these provinces pass from the civil into the hands of the military department.'

He then wrote to each of the brigade commanders in turn, enclosing copies of his letter. He hoped that the realisation of his firmness would stop the expected action.

He thought this might have happened where Smith's Second Brigade, in the front line, was concerned, for he heard nothing more from Smith for the time being.

Sir Robert Barker, commanding the Third Brigade, acted with determination. He assembled his officers and harangued them on their duty. But they merely replied that they were in it with the officers from other brigades.

It was Sir Robert Fletcher of the First Brigade who acted the most strangely. He seemed, on the surface, to be as staunch as the other two commanders, yet he forwarded to Clive the complaints of his dissident officers.

Clive immediately ordered all the spare officers from Madras to be sent to Bengal, only to hear that the rebellious officers had been in touch with their companions in Madras, and had told them to refuse to sail.

Clive then offered commissions to the free merchants of Calcutta. Only two came forward. The feeling against Clive was so great among the merchants, deprived of their capacity to pillage, that they would support anyone in opposition to him. A sum of £16,000 was mysteriously donated, from the same sources, to the rebellious officers.

Suddenly Smith on the frontier found himself in a terrible position. The reason he had not written to Clive was because he had not received his letter and knew nothing of the plot. Then, with the Mahrattas expected to attack, he learnt that a large number of his officers were about to resign on 1 May, and only continue as volunteers until 15 May.

In this one case, Clive made an exception. In the absolute last resort, Smith could negotiate with the rebellious officers; but only if it meant saving the battle.

Clive had now come to the conclusion that the centre of the mutiny lay in Sir Robert Fletcher's First Brigade. There was something oddly two-faced about Fletcher. He had not shown the genuine alarm of Smith or Barker's fierce loyalty. While seeming to condemn the threatened mutiny, he had at the same time pushed it on its way.

Clive determined to confront the whole of the First Brigade in person.

He left Sykes to carry on the business at Moorshedabad, and travelling with Carnac made for First Brigade headquarters at Monghyr.

But first, he sent forward a few reliable officers.

They acted with great speed and subtlety. They told all concerned that Clive was on his way, and that nothing would make him yield.

Then they changed their line of attack. How could officers they said, treat Clive in this way after he, Clive, had just given up £70,000 of his private money to form a fund for indigent officers?

The officers at Monghyr promptly replied that they had never heard of any such fund; Sir Robert Fletcher having, it appeared, 'forgotten' to inform them of Clive's generosity. This revelation led to the further interesting one that Sir Robert Fletcher was, despite his assurances to the contrary, the leader of the mutiny.

Clive arrived at Monghyr and heard from Fletcher himself that he had known about the projected mutiny since January, even though he had said nothing about it until April.

Realising that this was not the moment for a confrontation with his commander, Clive made no comment upon this extraordinary piece of behaviour.

Instead he called the troops together, explained what had happened and doubled the pay for the sepoys for May and June.

That, as far as the First Brigade was concerned, was that.

Then he moved on to Bangipore. But Barker's firmness had already made a number of the dissident officers change their minds. The rest were easily rounded up and arrested.

The situation on the Second Brigade waiting for the Mahrattas to attack had now reached a desperate stage.

On 6 May, all the officers in camp, except two, put in their resignations. Some were to take immediate effect. These, despite the threat of imminent attack by the Mahrattas, Smith sent immediately back to Calcutta.

The rest said that they would stay on until 1 June.

Smith retorted that he did not want them, and said that he would prefer to transfer the confidence he once had in them to the sepoys instead.

So curious was their conception of honour, that the rebellious officers immediately complained that he had insulted them.

Smith merely replied that the first point of honour of a soldier was his duty.

In the end, by sending half his officers away to Calcutta, he managed to hold the rest by example and threat. While at Allahabad, another Smith, a major this time who was in command of the fortress, moved his old battalion of sepoys, 104 miles in 54 hours, just in time to prevent a walk-out of both officers and men.

The rebellion was over. Clive, Barker and the two Smiths between them had frustrated the mutineers. Many of the rebellious officers tried to get their commissions back. Many were almost in tears. They were allowed to do so but had to sign on for a further three years with the Company, and to agree to give a year's notice of their intention to resign.

The ring-leaders were cashiered. None were shot, possibly because of an ambiguity in their contracts.

Sir Robert Fletcher was also court-martialed, found guilty and cashiered.

Thus the threat of mutiny disappeared.

In a little over a year Clive had deprived the Select Committee of its powers, taken over Bengal, signed treaties of friendship with the Nawab of Oudh and the Emperor Shah Alam, placated the civil service and put down an army rebellion.

Rarely has one man achieved so much in reforms in so short a time.

Chapter 17

The Most Famous of the Nabobs

The strain of dealing with one problem after another again affected Clive's health. Beneath his tough exterior was a hypersensitive person. The weakness caused by that early childhood illness had never left him. In moments of stress he could hardly move for the pain. The climate and the over-spiced food made it worse. Only by taking more and more massive doses of drugs, particularly morphia and laudanum, could he go on.

He had his own supplier of drugs in Calcutta, a man who could and did produce for him the purest and best morphia in the East.

He was dosing himself heavily even before the nerve-racking and awful officers' mutiny. Travelling, in the appalling damp heat – it was so hot that Smith's European regiment did not at first march with the Second Brigade from Allahabad – he only kept going because of his determination, the drugs and his hope that he would soon be on his way back to England, Margaret and his family.

He had already, in 1765, written to the Court Directors in London telling them that he intended resigning the Governorship as soon as he had completed the tasks they had set him. The Court, in a letter dated March 1766, begged him to stay at least another year in India.

But by the time the letter reached him, the officers' mutiny was over, and he was back in Calcutta, really desperately ill with a liver complaint.

Any continuation of effort at the present high level of concentration would in all probability have killed him.

The Governor-designate, Verelst, had had time to learn

his job. In Sykes, Cartier and Warren Hastings Clive felt that he had that new kind of administrator he wanted. Even Sullivan back in London had been finally defeated for the Chairmanship of the Company.

It looked as if the old pirate days were over. He felt that the East India Company had at last realised its responsibilities, and, like him, could see that Bengal was not just a place for unscrupulous get-rich-quick adventurers to operate in, but a country with its own traditions, aspirations and way of life.

If he still had doubts about the ability of the Company to achieve this, he kept them to himself.

On 16 January 1767 he made his last appearance at the Council, and after begging the members to live up to their new responsibilities left Calcutta for England on 29 January 1767.

He sailed on board the *Britannia* with his old friend Carnac, having appointed Colonel Richard Smith, the unshakable commander of the Second Brigade, Commander-in-Chief in Carnac's place.

Clive had always, up till then, been unlucky in his sea journeys. From the very first, they invariably took much longer than they need. They usually took a year. But, on the other hand, they often did him good. The sea air seemed to revive him; his stricken liver gained strength. The gallstone that was growing ever more painful became quiescent.

But this journey did not take as long as usual. He landed on 14 July, hardly six months after leaving Calcutta. In the past, he had fretted at the slowness of the sailing ships that had heaved and groaned beneath his feet. On this occasion, it might have been better if he had taken his usual year. He was still far from well.

But the next day he was in London, back in his splendid house in Berkeley Square, reunited once more with Margaret and his family. There was, too, his country house at Walcot, and the waters of Bath to bring him back to health.

He had once again a hero's welcome; but it was a

17a Caricature of Clive on an elephant. Authorship is unknown. One of the characters is marked 'Carnac'. He was Clive's Commander-in-Chief and close friend in Bengal at the time of the officers' mutiny. *(India Records Office)*

17b Indian in palanquin, such as the one Omi Chand arrived in for his 'undeceiving'. These were the recognised means of conveyance of the wealthy Indians. Many of the European businessmen, or nabobs, had especially elaborate palanquins constructed to rival the Indians in their style of life. *(India Records Office)*

18 Shah Alam's military camp, 1765. Another of the special Court paintings carried out automatically by the accredited Court painters. They occupied relatively the same position as cameramen today. *(India Records Office)*

19 Commodore Wilson's flagship engaging the French ship, St. Louis in the Bay of Bengal 1758. Wilson commanded one of the East Indiamen when the Dutch fleet unexpectedly attacked. 'Private armies' were a feature of the times. The East India Company controlled a navy far superior to that of many sovereign states. (*National Maritime Museum*)

20a Idealised impression of Clive at the Battle of Plassey. Artists had very little idea of what life in India was like, and tended to draw pictures based on European-style fighting—with a consequent severe lack of 'reality'. *(Radio Times Hulton Picture Library)*

20b Clive's meeting with Mir Jaffar after the Battle of Plassey. Another 'idealised' and extremely inaccurate representation of the meeting. The artist was anyhow more interested in obtaining a pleasing grouping of his subjects than being historically exact. *(Radio Times Hulton Picture Library)*

somewhat muted hero's welcome.

The King and Queen, it was true, showed every satisfaction at seeing him back; but the King did not, as Clive expected, change his Irish peerage to an English one.

Pitt, Earl of Chatham, was in office again, but though expressing the same admiration for Clive as before, did not offer him any political position. Clive's health would not have made it possible to accept a post, but he would have liked the offer, or the suggestion of one.

The Court of Directors had erected a statue of him at their headquarters in India House (as also of General Stringer Lawrence and Admiral Pocock) but they showed a somewhat carping spirit when once again the subject of his jaghire came up.

There was no question of taking away, as Sullivan had wanted to do, the £30,000 a year quit-rent Mir Jaffar had awarded him. But when it was suggested that he should enjoy it for another ten years, some of the Directors had not been as enthusiastic as they might have been. There had been suggestions that it should be cut to a smaller sum.

Though eventually, at a General Court called together shortly after his return, the extension was agreed unanimously, the knowledge of the earlier hesitations still rankled.

Then there was trouble with the Court of Proprietors of the East India Company, who through their shares owned the Company's assets. Many of his old enemies, the men he had kicked out of Bengal before they could make their fortunes, bought shares in the Company, with the express intention of making trouble.

When Clive had succeeded in getting Shah Alam's permission to be responsible for Bengal's finances, the East India Company's wealth had immediately increased. This coming of peace had also improved the Company's financial position.

There was a demand among the shareholders in London to increase the dividend to $12\frac{1}{2}$ per cent. Though Clive himself was, in fact, in favour of this, neither the Court of

Directors nor the Government wanted it.

However the agreement was carried.

The Government immediately brought in an Act reducing the amount to 10 per cent, and at the same time imposed a £400,000 levy on the Company, as it was doing so well.

Clive was furiously opposed to the levy. He wrote very strongly on the matter to the Government. Several Cabinet Ministers were very annoyed indeed at the tone of Clive's letters.

He became even more angry with the Court of Proprietors, who owned the business and controlled the Court of Directors, when he discovered that they had decided not to proceed against the members of the Bengal Council Clive had sacked.

The Court of Directors was determined to bring these officials to justice for disobeying its order not to accept presents from the Indian rulers. But the Court of Proprietors was still annoyed with the members of the Court of Directors for having opposed the $12\frac{1}{2}$ per cent interest rate. Though Clive had supported the increase, and was not therefore directly involved, most of those who had opposed the increased rates were friends and supporters of his. It gave Clive's enemies among the shareholders a chance to attack him in yet another way.

At the same time, there was a general and deeper sense of unease and crticism in the country. Clive was considered a Nabob. The country was full of these merchants just returned from the East with their fabulous fortunes. These men were often extremely ostentatious in their way of living, and in the use of their power.

For the most part, they were the sons of the fairly impoverished landed gentry. Their natural position in society was that of somebody on the very fringe. They might, through a distant cousin, be vaguely connected with somebody of importance in the tight small snobbish circles of the time. But they had no position in themselves.

Then, suddenly, with their vast fortunes, they were able

to compete with the richest and most powerful in the land. They could and did aspire to the political positions traditionally held by the great political families. They upset the careful social structure of society; and were consequently feared, hated and, at the same time, despised by the very people they were trying to make their friends. The Nabobs were the Nouveaux Riches of the time, the ostentatious representatives of a new class that was spiralling vigorously upward.

Clive, the most famous of the Nabobs, was the most envied. His friend, Pigot, was another, as were other Company men, but Clive was the one to be attacked. There were no laws of libel. Anyone, with even a few pounds to spare, could hire a hack-journalist and his printer and publish a news sheet, as inaccurate and defamatory as he pleased.

These news sheets were quickly passed from hand to hand. They were eagerly read, for they formed the basis for that snide gossip that was so much enjoyed in the candle-heated drawing-rooms of society ladies. Nor were their victims slow to retaliate. Hiring other journalists, or even the same, they would produce equally offensive counter-blasts. And so the battle of the news sheets would continue, growing more and more violent, and further and further away from any possible truth; until eventually the episode was submerged by the arrival of an even more scurrilous scandal.

Clive's enemies, particularly those he had made in Bengal were quicker to make use of this means of attacking him. They issued pamphlet after pamphlet against him, underlining over and over again the point that whereas he made a huge fortune in Bengal, he would not allow those who followed him to do the same.

His doctors had hoped that this return to the more moderate climate of England and visits to Bath would complete his cure. But this was not so. As the problems and attacks mounted, so his bile trouble increased. Even his wife's care could not prevent him worrying and showing by bursts of irritable anger how much events were hurting him, and these hurts were translated into more and more violent liver attacks.

There was, they said, nothing for it but a visit to a spa in France, where the waters were famous for complaints of his kind.

On 19 January 1768, he wrote to his friend Call at Madras:

'I have suffered so much ever since my arrival in England, that I have not been able to interfere so much with public affairs as I could wish; and the bilious disorder is at last arrived at such a height, that there seems no other remedy but that of going to the south without delay; and in two hours I hope to be getting into my carriage for that purpose.'

He adds later in the same letter, with rather touching pride, the fact that so many of his family are now Members of Parliament: 'We shall come very strong into Parliament this year – seven without opposition, probably one more; Lord Clive, Shrewsbury; Richard Clive, Montgomery; William and George Clive, Bishop's Castle; John Walsh, Worcester; Henry Strachey, Pontefract; and Edmund Maskelyne, probably either for Whitechurch or Cricklade.'

The Nabobs were on the march.

In the meantime, Clive's little party, consisting of himself, Margaret, her brother Edmund Maskelyne and three others arrived safely in Paris.

From here on 9 February he wrote to Verelst saying that the change of climate had already done him a lot of good.

From Paris he went on to Lyons and then Montpellier.

In April 1768, he wrote to his secretary, Strachey: 'I suffer in the manner I did on board the *Britannia,* both from the bile and from my former nervous complaint, but not more, which convinces me the roots of both disorders still remain, and I much fear I must be unhappy as long as I live, tho' I am certain there is nothing mortal in either of them, and, in all probability, I shall drag on a miserable life for 15 or 20 years longer, as I have already done since the year 1752.'

He continued to take an interest in parliamentary affairs, particularly Indian ones whilst he was abroad, and was incensed to hear that there was a move to reinstate Sir Robert Fletcher to the affairs of the Company. Clive could never forgive Sir Robert for having been the invidious leader of the officers' mutiny in Bengal. Fletcher even published a pamphlet claiming that his court-martial had not been fair. Clive was restrained, only with the greatest difficulty, from replying.

From Montpellier he returned to Paris, and then paid a short visit to the spa. He found the place so utterly boring that, despite his doctors' and friends' advice, he refused to stay a moment longer. His doctors tried to persuade him to return south and spend the winter in the South of France. But there had been a General Election in England, and his party was much stronger. There were problems to be dealt with both in Parliament and the East India Company that needed his attention.

Besides he felt very much better, and resented being side-tracked from public life at what seemed to him an important moment.

He and his party returned to England in August 1768.

But despite his assurances of improved good health, he had to spend much of his time at Bath. So that he was not able to 'interfere' in public affairs as much as he would have liked. Indeed, his protector in Parliament, George Grenville, advised him against hasty action where the East India Company was concerned; even to the extent of not opposing the reinstatement of Sir Robert Fletcher.

However, he found much to keep himself busy. Like most Nabobs, he went into the property business. Property gave a man power. It helped him with his political ambitions. It was, more than money, the outward and visible sign of success.

He had never had any wish to turn Styche into his main seat. The amount of land surrounding it was far too small, and his neighbours would certainly not sell. Shropshire was anyhow far too damp for him.

However, to please his family he had 'improved' the property a few years earlier in 1762. This had meant pulling down – the favourite device of the 'developer' in whatever century he lives – the half-timbered house, then considered old-fashioned, and replacing it, higher up on a small hill, by a hideous square building, redeemed only by the fine plaster-work and chimney-pieces inside. To-day it is an 'apartment' house.

He already had Lord Ancram's London house (now 45 Berkeley Square, the only house of that period still standing). He had, at first, rented it for £600 a year, but in 1764 had bought it for £10,500, and then under the guidance of the architect, Sir William Chambers, spent over £5,000 in improving it, adding spacious rooms for his secretaries and servants, as Margaret was always concerned (an unusual trait at the time) about the welfare of the servants.

He also had Walcot in Shropshire, close to the Welsh border. This was, on the whole, a political move and allowed him to control the Bishop's Castle electorate. However, Chambers again 'improved' the property, as he had done at Styche. This time, however, he did not pull down the half-timbered building, but hid most of it behind a Doric portico and a parapet, and replaced the old-fashioned Elizabethan lozenge windows with the then modern sash windows.

But Clive's main ambition was to buy a large property within a radius of fifty miles of London. He made a bid for Chilham Castle in Kent but the deal fell through. Clive was as tough a negotiator in the property as in the commercial world. He had no intention of paying more than was necessary.

He heard that the Duchess of Newcastle wanted to sell Claremont in Surrey. She was the widow of the Duke of Newcastle who had been responsible for him losing his first seat in Parliament. But Clive had not felt any rancour. In fact, he had lent Newcastle money and already held a mortgage on the house. Because of this, he was able to buy it for £25,000 instead of the £40,000 the Duchess was asking.

No sooner had he bought it, than he immediately had the old house pulled down; not, in this case, because it wasn't grand enough, for it was by Vanbrugh, but because it was damp. One of the reasons for moving to Surrey was to escape the damp Shropshire air. There was no point therefore in keeping up what he intended to be his main country seat, however grand it might be, if he could not live in it.

The new building, unlike the one at Styche, was both comfortable and elegant. It was the combined work of three talented men: John Soane, then a young man, Henry Holland and the famous Capability Brown. It was original because it contained an unusually high basement, another example of Margaret's insistence that the servants quarters should be at least habitable.

It had also a huge grey marble bath costing over £300, a part of the medical equipment his doctors recommended. He spent large sums of money on it. He had a marble floor installed in the hall, and insisted on the library being made of rosewood. He engaged famous artists just to come to Claremont and advise on this matter or the other. It was intended that the great dining-room, designed by Capability Brown himself, was to have had a series of paintings by Benjamin West, illustrating Clive's moments of triumph. Even the great Gobelin firm of France was approached with an idea of producing a set of tapestries celebrating his victories.

But, in fact, he never lived at Claremont, although he used to stay at the Home Farm from time to time to supervise the construction of the big house. It is now a girls' school.

Oddly enough, it was in a damp area of the country that he found most happiness. This was at the fourth of his country houses: Oakly Park near Ludlow. It was not a particularly grand house at the time, and for once Clive made very few alterations (many were made subsequently by his descendants), but it had a magnificent setting and it suited Margaret and their growing children. Clive himself indeed began to like it so much that he regretted spending so much on Claremont. It is the only house still in the possession of a descendant of his: the present Earl of Plymouth.

With all this extra wall-space to fill, it was natural that Clive should start buying paintings. But he moved with his usual caution until he was ready, and then bought rapidly. He engaged Benjamin West and William Patoun to advise him. In February 1771 he bought eighteen pictures from Christie's, including a £546 Dolci. By the middle of March he added a further eleven, and by April seven more; making thirty-six paintings in a little over two months. But he paid little more than £50 for most of them.

Faking pictures or attributing them to other painters was popular at the time. Despite Patoun and West's efforts, Clive did not escape the practice. He bought an 'Entombment' from the unscrupulous Sir James Wright under the impression that it was a Van Dyck. West said it was a Luca Giordano; but Clive told his secretary, Henry Strachey, to continue the bidding, and eventually got it, whatever it really was, for a bargain price.

Of more lasting controversy was the Canaletto he bought for £147 in 1773. It showed a view of Verona, a typical Canaletto subject, but not perhaps as sharp in detail as some. Subsequently, experts declared that it was a Bellotto. The arguments continue to this day. Recently Charles Wilson, Chairman of Sotheby's, went to Powis Castle where it is kept, and told the Countess of Powis that, in his opinion, it was a genuine Canaletto, 'Not', he added, 'that it matters very much. I could get you £150,000 for it whether it was a Canaletto or a Bellotto.' The Countess replied however that the picture was not for sale.

Though Benjamin West, then in his middle thirties, had been engaged to paint the series of large paintings illustrating Clive's glories, his main service was in fact the purchase of these paintings, including two fine Claudes.

The Claudes are still in the family's possession and are to be found at Oakly Park, along with the only commemorative canvas Benjamin West completed: Clive receiving the Diwani of Bengal from the Shah Alam at Allahabad in 1765. West, as was normal at the time, took a great deal of historical liberties with his subject. Although the real event took place in Clive's tent, West has transferred it to a luxurious palace. Even more inaccurate is the inclusion in the painting of two Englishmen, friends of Clive's at a later period, who were nowhere near Allahabad at the time.

But then Clive was, by his own estimation alone, worth over £500,000 (£5,000,000 today) by then; having by prudent investment and purchases almost doubled the capital he brought back with him. Even if he wasn't the richest man in the country he was believed to be. If a Nabob couldn't please a couple of friends by putting them into a painting, what could he do?

In the meantime, a new danger began to appear. Sullivan had never forgiven Clive for being the cause of his defeat at the Court of Directors. Nor had he and his friends given up hope of returning to power. Johnstone, whom Clive had sacked in Calcutta, had bought shares in the East India Company, and as a shareholder and member of the Court of Proprietors, could also threaten Clive. Vansittart, once a friend of Clive's but now, because he had joined with Sullivan, his enemy, still had hopes of being reappointed Governor of Bengal, where, as usual when Clive was away, conditions had returned to the bad old days.

But Clive was aware of the danger. The Directors, he declared, seemed only concerned to 'strip the company of all they can'. Nor was the Government any better. All it cared about was the next election, and how not to lose power.

He saw, with a desolate insight, his country slipping to disaster, both in India and the wider world.

In a letter to Claud Russell in Bengal on 10 February 1769, he writes with prophetic clearness: 'We are drawing very fast towards a dangerous crisis, from which we can only be extricated by some first-rate genius, and where to find that genius does not appear at present. Our wide and extended possessions are becoming too great for the Mother country, or for our abilities, to manage. America is making great strides towards independency; so is Ireland. The East Indies also, I think, cannot remain long to us, if our present constitution is not altered.'

In April of that year, Sullivan and his friends were successful in regaining positions within the Court of Directors. An attempt to get Vansittart reappointed Governor-General was defeated by Clive, but he had, in exchange, to agree to the sending of a powerful Commission consisting of Vansittart, and two of Clive's supporters, Forde and Scrafton, to Bengal. Its task was to reform the Indian administration.

The Commission, however, was fated never to reach its destination. It sailed on the *Aurora* frigate. She called in at the Cape of Good Hope, and sailed north-east for India. She was never seen or heard of again.

In the April elections of 1770 and again, 1771, Sullivan and his party held their advantage. Clive was more and more discouraged, and spoke frequently of retiring into private life, and taking no further part in either the Company's affairs or Parliament.

In Bengal matters had reached crisis point again. Verelst had been well-meaning, but lacked strength of character. He was succeeded in January 1770 by Cartier. His mildness and weakness could not deal with one of the worst famines Bengal had ever endured. One third of the population died from sickness and starvation.

Unable to take the terrible responsibility any more, Cartier resigned.

The only alternative was Warren Hastings. For some reason, Clive had never had a high opinion of Warren Hastings. Perhaps he could not recognise in another the qualities he had himself: courage and statesmanship. Certainly, his choices for the Governorship had all been disastrous: Vansittart, Verelst and Cartier.

Now, because of the pressures of those friends of his who knew Warren Hastings, he agreed to his appointment. But even so, he still had his misgivings.

In a letter, written from his Berkeley Square home on 1 August 1771 congratulating Warren Hastings on his appointment, Clive still felt it necessary to write: '. . but I thought I discovered in you a diffidence in your own judgement, and too great an easiness of disposition, which may subject you insensibly to be *led* where you ought to *guide.*'

It would have been as inapposite for Warren Hastings to say the same of Clive. They were perhaps the only two men in the country who could *not* be led, and who *could* guide. But they appear not to have seen this in each other.

Chapter 18

Astonished at My Own Moderation

It started quite innocently.

On 21 January 1772, Parliament met again. Among the measures announced by the King in the speech from the throne was the proposal that new laws were to be introduced 'for supplying defects or remedying abuses' in the administration in India.

Clive approved of the introduction of these laws. He had, in fact, been in consultation with Lord North, the Prime Minister, and Lord Rochford, Secretary of State, on this question. This, despite the fact that he was in opposition to Lord North and his party. But whenever any Indian matters came up he was prepared to give his advice to whoever needed it. One of his complaints was that hardly anybody, whether in Parliament or not, knew what was really going on, or even seemed to care; and did not ask for his views often enough.

Of course, the newspapers had been attacking the Nabobs and him in general more violently than ever. There were pseudopious articles on the iniquity of men amassing huge fortunes in the East. There were 'financial' articles showing how these fortunes could and did, by the introduction of unexpected wealth, disrupt the economy of the country. And there were the usual scurrilous pamphlets pushed around from hand to hand, full of libellous attacks on his person and his family.

But Clive, like any man of position, had grown accustomed to this stream of abuse, and paid no attention to it.

More serious, however, had been a curious little incident that had taken place a fortnight before the assembly of Parliament.

Without warning, he received an official letter dated 7 January 1772 from the Secretary of the East India Company informing him, in dry unemotional tones, that the Court of Directors had been sent a number of papers containing accusations against Clive's management of the Company's affairs whilst he was in Bengal. They accused him specifically of manipulating various monopolies in cotton, diamonds, gold, salt, betel-nut, tobacco and other commodities to his profit. He was asked to comment upon the accusations as soon as convenient.

It did not take Clive long to realise that this was the work of Sullivan and the others who were his enemies.

He wrote at once to the Court of Directors, pointing out that the papers were anonymous, that the Court had not even told him why they had been sent to him, and what he was expected to do about them.

He added that his service to the Company was recorded in the Company books for all to see; and that that record alone was enough to refute the anonymous charges.

Four and a half years had now gone by since his return to England and if there had been anything in his behaviour detrimental to the Company or even puzzling to the Court, he would surely have been called to account before now.

That, as far as he was concerned, was that.

An M.P. called Vane, seconding the Address in the House of Commons, suggested that a new law should be passed making it impossible for East India Company officials to make huge personal fortunes. He felt that the Court of Directors had not sufficient control over their own servants to enforce these regulations; and that, if the present practices continued, the whole of Bengal might be lost.

But no one took up Vane's suggestion.

Then, two months later, on 30 March 1772, Sullivan made his next move. Besides being now the Deputy Chairman of the Court of Directors he was also a Member of Parliament.

He gave notice of a motion to introduce a bill 'for the better regulation of the affairs of the East India Company, and of their servants in India, and for the due administration of justice in Bengal.'

He gave his reasons for wishing to introduce this bill and spoke of '. . . charges made or insinuated, against former Governors of the country.'

This was a clear reference to Clive.

Clive immediately decided to take up Sullivan's challenge. Since the charges against him had now, thanks to the newspapers and pamphlets, been made public, the sooner he refuted them the better.

His speech was a long one. It occupied thirty-four columns of Almon's Parliamentary History for 1772, revised and published by T. Hansard in 1813.

It was, according to Pitt (now Earl of Chatham) who listened to it, the finest he had ever heard.

Clive explained how he had received the cryptic letter from Mitchell, the Secretary of the East India Company, setting out the anonymous accusations. He gave his reply and then dealt with each accusation in turn.

There were four of them; and they all referred to his third visit to Bengal.

It was stated first of all that he ran a monopoly of cotton. To this he replied that the cotton trade was not his profession. His line had been military and political. 'I owe all I have in the world to my having been at the head of an army; and as to cotton – I know no more about it than the Pope of Rome.'

Then he was accused of trading in diamonds. He pointed out that there were only two ways for a servant of the Company to transmit money. One was by receiving bills on the Company of the other by purchasing diamonds.

After he had successfully negotiated the Diwani or agreement to run the Bengal finances, the Company was so rich it wasn't possible to draw bills on it.

In order to send the money from the quit-rent Mir Jaffar had given him, he sent an agent 'into a distant and independent country to make purchases of diamonds.' He pointed out that the purchases were not clandestine, that the diamonds had been registered, and that he had paid duty on them, adding ruefully that the duty turned out at three per cent, 'worse than bills of exchange upon the Company.' That, he declared, was all he knew about the monopoly of diamonds.

The third charge accused him of fraud in the establishment of a gold coinage in Bengal.

It was, he declared, a subject completely outside his sphere. He knew nothing about the mixture of alloys and metals.

The Select Committee had decided to introduce a gold coinage in Bengal in order to prevent silver coins, the only currency in use, from being drained off to China. He did not know whether the plan succeeded, as he left Bengal before it was put into operation. All he could say was that he did not receive a farthing from it, and that he never sent a single rupee or gold mohur to be coined in his life.

The fourth charge had, he said, an extraordinary title – 'A monopoly of salt, betel-nut and tobacco, and other commodities, which occasioned the late famine.'

How a monopoly of salt, betel-nut and tobacco in 1765 and 1766 could occasion a want of rain and scarcity of rice in the year 1770 was, he declared, beyond his comprehension. He then went on to explain that whether the monopoly was right or not, he had always acted under the instructions of the Court of Directors.

Had he left the matter there, it is likely that nothing would have been heard of Sullivan's accusations; but Clive could not resist the temptation to use the occasion for a general attack both on the Court of Directors and the Government. As he had written to Russell and to many other friends, he was extremely concerned at the way the Government was mishandling its overseas possessions. Perhaps he hoped that he could, even now, make North realise that unless the Government adopted a more liberal attitude in both America and the East, everything would be lost.

To Chatham, listening under the gallery, this may have been the finest speech he had heard. But to Clive's friends, it seemed that he had never spoken with more detriment to himself.

For North was not one to welcome criticism, especially when it came from the opposition. By denouncing the Government for its lack of policy, its deficiency in courage and foresight, and its greed in seizing as much of the Company's money as possible, Clive was only speaking the truth. But truth, in politics, is a dangerous thing.

When he sat down, Governor Johnstone, a brother of the Johnstone Clive had sacked in Calcutta, then stood up. He spoke with considerable violence against Clive, and even attacked him over his generosity of setting up his Fund from Mir Jaffar's personal legacy.

Though the violent way Johnstone spoke defeated much of the harm he wanted to do, Sullivan's motion was passed without a division, and set down for 13 April.

But at this stage, the flamboyant political adventurer Colonel Burgoyne appeared on the scene. With apparent impartiality he pointed out that it was pointless voting on a bill without examining the whole problem carefully. He proposed that a Select Committee should be appointed 'to inquire into the nature, state and condition of the East India Company, and of the British affairs in the East Indies.'

As Burgoyne was a friend of Sullivan's, the whole manoeuvre had all the appearances of a device designed to bring Clive in front of what amounted to a Grand Jury of the House of Commons.

A number of speakers, among them Edmund Burke, protested strongly against such a course, but they were overruled. The Select Committee was set up. It was to consist of thirty-one members. Sullivan's bill was dropped after the second reading.

Burgoyne himself was chairman of the Committee. Johnstone was a member of it, as were a number of the other anti-Clive men. In fact the majority of the Committee was hostile to him. Clive himself was one of the members, so was his close friend and former secretary, Henry Strachey.

In one sense, Sullivan and his Court of Directors had made a mistake. The whole of the East India Company's handling of its trade in India was now common talk. It did not take long for people to realise that the Company itself and the way it underpaid its employees was to blame. It was also, without realising it, allowing the control of its own affairs to pass to the Government.

But it was too late now. While prevaricating, in order to delay a decision in the present session, it increased its pressure on Clive.

It was no longer a question of scrutinising, as in Sullivan's motion, the events in Bengal of four or five years ago. Now the Committee ranged over the whole of Clive's activities in India both before and after Plassey.

Clive, again true to character, never hesitated. He had taken on greater odds before and won. He would win again. Let them ask him any question they liked. He would answer them all.

Yes, he had cheated Omi Chand with the red and white treaties. He had forged Admiral Watson's signature. In the same set of circumstances, he would do both again. He would do them a hundred times over.

Yes, he had received enormous presents from Mir Jaffar; but at that time there was nothing in the law forbidding him to do so.

At the end of one of these long probing sessions, he turned on Burgoyne and his thinly disguised judges and said, cuttingly, 'Am I not rather deserving of praise for the moderation which marked my proceedings? Consider the situation in which the victory at Plassey had placed me. A great prince was dependent on my pleasure; an opulent city lay at my mercy; its richest bankers bid against each other for my smiles; I walked through vaults which were thrown open to me alone, piled on either hand with gold and jewels! Mr Chairman, at this moment I stand astonished at my own moderation!'

Sullivan and Burgoyne between them were not slow in

circulating the findings of the Select Committee. They hoped to influence the public against Clive. The effect was somewhat different. They found a good deal of support among the less intelligent members of the population, particularly if they came from the poorer sections. Many were envious of Clive's wealth and were happy to see the mud slung at him.

But among the more intelligent, and therefore more important sections of the public the reaction was rather different. These people remembered Clive's great victories. They admired his frankness admitting the charges, and his courage in standing up to his accusers. They began to perceive that it was not Clive, but the East India Company that was at fault.

The Government was far from happy. It wanted very much an investigation into the affairs of the East India Company, as this private Company now had Governmental responsibilities. There was a feeling that the time would soon come when the Government would have to have some control in the Company's management.

But instead of a general review of the East India Company's affairs, the Select Committee had degenerated into a witch-hunt against Clive. Although Clive might not be a member of North's party, the last thing the Prime Minister wanted was for him to be discredited.

War with America was coming closer every day. Clive was still Chatham's 'heaven-born' general. He was indeed, now that Wolfe was dead, the only general of any stature in the country at all. Already Clive was being ear-marked as a possible Commander-in-Chief of any forces to be sent to America.

Not that North was pressing very firmly for this. It was not in his character to do so. He wanted at all costs to be popular and loved by all. He longed to be left in peace to enjoy life.

Clive, who was constantly and acutely aware of the threat to the thinly protected British possessions overseas, drew up for the Prime Minister a lengthy and very detailed plan embracing the complete reorganisation of the Indian Government at home and abroad.

But North, though worried, was not very interested.

In a letter from Walcot, addressed to his secretary Strachey, Clive wrote with a certain ironic bitterness: 'Lord North when I saw him, seemed industriously to avoid entering upon the subject of India affairs; and I do verily believe, from sheer indolence of character, he wishes to leave everything to Providence and the Directors.'

That was the trouble. Whether it was India, Ireland or America, there was a general awareness that a crisis was approaching; but nowhere was there any clear sense of purpose, any single-minded leader.

It would have to take the French Revolution to bring the Younger Pitt to the fore, and for the country to have, once again, a strong sense of direction.

In the meantime, North bumbled on.

The King, who also supported Clive and wanted to show his approval, had made the famous Nabob a Knight of the Order of the Bath on 15 June, soon after Parliament had risen earlier that year.

In September, the Earl of Powis, the Lord-Lieutenant of Shropshire had died. Because Clive now had large possessions in the county he felt that he was entitled to be appointed to the position, but, with the Select Committee attacking him, he did not want to ask North or his Ministers for any favour.

His friends, including Strachey, suggested that he should short-cut the Prime Minister and go direct to the King. But Clive refused to do this as he felt that the many Members of the House of Commons would disapprove, and turn against him in his struggle with Sullivan.

However, his name had already been mentioned to the King. North, as usual, did not have any strong opinions one way or another, and eventually agreed to forward Clive's name.

On 9 October 1772, Clive was formally appointed Lord-Lieutenant of Shropshire. Later the Lord-Lieutenancy of

Montgomeryshire was also added.

The King and the Prime Minister were not the only people worried by the behaviour of the Select Committee. Those Directors who were not members of the Committee were extremely upset.

Since Clive had left Bengal, the usual decline had set in. In the normal course, the Directors would have appealed to him to go out and rescue the Company once more. But with Sullivan attacking him through the Select Committee, this was impossible.

The Company was now, through mismanagement in Bengal and further internal warfare at Madras, in a desperate financial situation. Trade had come almost to a stop. Corruption and bribery was once again on the increase. More than ever before, each man was out to make his own fortune.

By October 1772, there was the huge deficit of £1,293,000 to be faced. Bank loans had not raised enough to cover this deficit. In the end, Sullivan announced that the Company had approached the Government in order to obtain a £1,000,000 loan.

On hearing of this request, the Lord of the Treasury merely referred them directly to Parliament; but North himself, who wanted the Government to gain control of the Company, decided that since the Select Committee was failing to do its duty a Secret Committee should be set up to report on the Company. It would have full power to inspect the Company's books and accounts, to report on the debts and credits of the Company, and to assess its worth.

The one thing the Directors most dreaded, direct Government control, seemed, by their own folly and Sullivan's vindictive attack on Clive, to be taking place. They appointed six supervisors to go out to India and see whether they could not bring stability to the Company's affairs before the Government could intervene.

But the Secret Committee moved with astonishing speed. Within a few days it produced a Special Report which recommended that a Bill should be introduced to restrain the

Company from sending out supervisors.

Edmund Burke commented dryly: 'Ministers, finding that the Select Committee of last year, a lawful wife publicly avowed, was barren, and had produced nothing, had taken a neat little snug one, which they called a Secret Committee, and that this was her first born. Indeed, from the singular expedition of this extraordinary delivery, I am apt to think she was pregnant before wedlock.'

One might have thought that this would be the end of the Select Committee, but Burgoyne was not easily defeated. He told the House that his Committee had discovered so much rottenness that he could not find a single spot in the whole business that wasn't completely corrupt. If the Secret Committee were to take the place of his Select Committee then he, Burgoyne, would look upon this as nothing less than a means of protecting the guilty.

This was enough for Lord North. His ambition was to avoid trouble. He hastily assured Burgoyne that he had no intention of doing anything of the sort.

Burgoyne was free to continue as inquisitor.

Thus a somewhat ludicrous position had now been reached. There were two Committees investigating, officially at least, the same matter: the Select Committee with thirty-one members, and the Secret Committee with thirteen.

Each had, in fact, a slightly different bias. The Secret Committee was collecting material for the Bill regulating the conduct of the East India Company that Lord North intended to bring in. Burgoyne and his Committee were still only interested in ruining Clive.

The two Committees had to find their material from the same source: India House. There was such an enormous amount of it that the newly formed Secret Committee just had not time to sift through it all. It had to take a good deal for granted from the East India Company clerks and the Select Committee.

It was not long before the two committees were working together; and the anti-Clive feelings of the Select Committee were absorbed by the Secret Committee.

To Clive, they were now both his enemies. So that when, on 3 May, North presented his Bill for the better management of the East India Company, Clive took the opportunity of repeating his old accusations against the Government and the Court of Directors.

He went even further, blaming, perhaps unwisely, nearly everyone in sight.

As one eye-witness wrote: 'He laid about him on all sides: he reprehended the Court of Directors, past and present: the Court of Proprietors, the citizens of London, the country gentlemen of England, the servants of the Company abroad, the Secret and Select Committees, the Opposition, the Minister and Ministry. He paid a compliment to the King.'

In his dangerous and difficult position, a more moderate approach might have been wiser. But Clive had always been bold. Once his mind was made up, he attacked with everything he had, whoever his enemies might be, or however strong.

The storm really broke a week later when Burgoyne at last laid his case before the House.

The same eye-witness as before wrote sorrowfully on this occasion: 'I was in the House all this day, and had the mortification to hear the transactions in India, for these last sixteen years, treated, without distinction, as a disgrace to this nation; but without the smallest idea of restoring to the injured natives of India the territories and revenues said to have been so unjustly acquired.'

Burgoyne omitted nothing. Everything could be traced back, he said, to the dethronement of Siraj-ud-dowla and the installation of Mir Jaffar. It was, he said, an act of the blackest perfidy. All the old business of the forged treaty, the falsifying of Watson's signature, the huge sums collected by the Calcutta Committee were brought up. Burgoyne did not care who or what he hurt, as long as he could add to the indictment. Rarely has a Member of Parliament run down his own country so much, in order to satisfy a personal spite against one man.

When he had finished speaking he placed three resolutions on record:

(1) 'That all acquisitions made under the influence of a military force, or by treaty with foreign Princes, do of right belong to the State.'

(2) 'That to appropriate acquisitions so made, to the private emolument of persons entrusted with any civil or military power of the State, is illegal.'

(3) 'That very great sums of money and other valuable property have been acquired in Bengal, from Princes and others of that country, by persons entrusted with the military and civil powers of the State, by means of such powers, which sums of money and valuable property have been appropriated to the private use of such persons.'

Just to make his intentions absolutely clear, Burgoyne stated that if these resolutions were carried, he would follow this up by a new resolution forcing anybody who had received large sums in this way to return the money.

As he accompanied this statement with a violent personal attack on Clive, it was quite obvious who he had in mind.

The resolutions were all carried. North himself and his Attorney-General voted for them. The Solicitor-General (Wedderburn) voted against.

Clive was now completely on his own.

21   Portrait of Clive. This is the official portrait painted by Dance. The original hangs at Powis Castle, and is in the possession of the Earl and Countess of Powis, who are descendants of Clive. *(National Portrait Gallery)*

LANSDOWNE HOUSE, Berkeley Square.

22　One of Clive's properties—Lansdowne House in Berkeley Square which was then a magnificent, almost rural district on the edge of London proper. Strict eighteenth-century planning gave it its elegant appearance. *(Radio Times Hulton Picture Library)*

23   Modern photograph of Claremont, Clive's Surrey home. Although he never lived to enjoy his new home, he spent much time, thought and money on its conversion. It is now a girl's school. (*Country Life*)

IEW of the ⋯ HOUSE of COM
⋯Arthur Onslow Esq⋯ Speaker of the House⋯

24 The House of Commons as it was in Clive's time. Although the number of members of Parliament
have increased since then, the procedures today are very much the same as they were then. *(Radio
Times Hulton Picture Library)*

Chapter 19

Primus in Indis

True to his promise, Burgoyne returned to the attack a few days later and laid the following resolution, mentioning Clive officially by name for the first time: 'That it appears to this House the Robert Lord Clive, Baron of Plassey in the Kingdom of Ireland, about the time of the deposing of Suraj-ud-doulah [sic] Nawab of Bengal, and the establishment of Mir Jaffar on the Masnad [throne], did, through the influence of the powers with which he was entrusted as a member of the Select Committee and Commander-in-Chief of the British forces, obtain and possess himself of two lakhs and 80,000 rupees, which sums were of the value, in English money, of £234,000; and that in so doing the said Robert Lord Clive abused the powers with which he was entrusted, to the evil example of the servants of the public.'

The real object of the Select Committee was at last revealed. Pushed on by the envy and hatred of Sullivan, Johnstone and the rest of the anti-Clive faction, its goal was simply the moral and financial ruin of the country's only capable general and far-seeing administrator.

The feeling that Burgoyne and his Committee had gone too far began to gain ground. It was one thing to investigate the general commercial practices of a possibly corrupt commercial company, but quite another to make a personal attack on one whose exploits at Arcot, Plassey and elsewhere were still vividly remembered. And, surely, the large areas of Bengal and the Carnatic which were now under British control were so largely because of him?

Clive replied to Burgoyne.

He pointed out once again that there was nothing in his

conduct of which he could be ashamed. The acceptance of presents had been an established practice of the East India Company for the past 150 years. He showed how he had changed the Company's position in India from that of a weak trader into the most effective power in the land. He again accepted full responsibility for the trick played on Omi Chand, adding: '. . . when the very existence of the Company was at stake, and the lives of the people so precariously situated, and so certain of being destroyed, it was a matter of true policy and of justice to deceive so great a villain.'

He spoke of the Dutch menace: 'I did not hesitate to give them battle; and in twenty-four hours I destroyed every ship they had, and their whole army was either killed, wounded or taken prisoner.'

He reminded the House that the Dutch had, at this time, most of his money.

He read congratulatory letters from the Directors, and referred to Chatham's high opinion.

He said that he felt that after all this, he could be allowed to enjoy his fortune uninterrupted, and unenvied by those not so rich as himself.

'. . . am I to be brought here like a criminal, and the very best parts of my conduct construed into crimes against the State? Is this the reward that is now held out to persons who have performed such important services to the country?'

A little later, he declared that everything he possessed was threatened, his credit gone, his position that of a bankrupt. He would have left nothing but the £500 a year that had been in his family for generations.

'But,' he continued, 'upon this I am content to live, and perhaps I shall find more real content of mind and happiness therein than in the trembling affluence of an unsettled fortune.'

He ended by reminding those present that when they decided upon his honour, their own was also at stake.

It was a powerful speech; and because it contained nothing except a plea for justice, and no personal attacks, it was more effective than his previous speeches.

The House was obviously disturbed and ill at ease. An adjournment was asked for and granted.

It was agreed that the debate should be continued on 21 May 1773.

The interval was spent in devising means of attenuating Burgoyne's violent resolution. One hopeful sign was that although it was aimed directly at Clive, it was couched in loose phrases. It might be possible, by suitable amendments, to deflect some of the venom from it.

When the matter came up for discussion again on 21 May, Clive made a brief speech, ending with the words 'Take my fortune, but save my honour' and then left the House.

More and more of the members of Parliament were beginning to realise that by voting for Burgoyne's three resolutions on 10 May, they were, in fact, taking sides in what was a bitter personal squabble. When it came to choosing between Sullivan on one side and Clive on the other, there could be no doubt who was the greater, indeed the better man. They had in fact, to put it crudely, been 'conned', and found themselves on the very point of condemning their greatest contemporary.

An M.P. called Stanley started the back-pedalling by moving that the words 'and that in so doing the said Robert Lord Clive abused the powers with which he was entrusted, to the evil example of the servants of the public, and to the dishonour and detriment of the State' should be omitted.

Richard Fuller, in seconding the motion, went further and proposed that the words 'through the influence of the powers with which he was entrusted, as a member of the Select Committee, and Commander-in-Chief of the British forces' should also be omitted.

There was a good deal of debate. North was in favour of keeping to the original violent form; so was Thurold his Attorney-General; but Wedderburn, the Solicitor-General, was against his colleagues. The House divided unevenly. Most of the Opposition supported Clive, even though he had been in favour of the Government's proposals to take over the East India Company.

In the end, the very much watered-down motion recording only that Clive had acquired a vast fortune, without any words of censure, was put to the House: 'That it appears to this House, that the Right Honourable Robert Lord Clive, Baron of Plassey in the Kingdom of Ireland, about the time of the deposition of Suraj-ud-dowlah, and the establishment of Meer Jaffier on the Masnad, [throne] did obtain and possess himself of 2 lakhs of rupees as Commander-in-Chief, a further sum of 2 lakhs and 80,000 rupees as member of the Select Committee, and a further sum of 16 lakhs or more under the denomination of a private donation; which sums, amounting together to 20 lakhs and 80,000 rupees, were of the value, in English money, of £234,000.'

This motion was carried by 155 votes to 95.

Burgoyne and his friends were furious. It would be impossible now to deprive Clive of his fortune.

They immediately put forward a new motion stating that 'Lord Clive did, in so doing, abuse the powers with which he was entrusted to the evil example of the servants of the public.'

But since the House had already deleted the similar, if much stronger, motion of censure, this new attempt to bring Clive down was thrown out.

No word of censure was in fact now contained in the resolution. Burgoyne, Sullivan and Johnstone had been completely beaten.

Not only that, but Wedderburn now went over to the attack and at 5 o'clock in the morning put forward a new motion. He proposed that the words 'Robert Lord Clive did at the same time render great and meritorious services to his country' should be added.

This was carried.

The extraordinary enquiry, which in fact was a trial, was over. The result was almost exactly opposite to what Sullivan expected. Far from condemning Clive, it merely recorded that he had made a fortune, and that in doing so had rendered his country 'great and meritorious services.'

The struggle was over. His name had been cleared. His fortune was safe. He could at last enjoy, without fear, his hard-earned affluence.

If the Select Committee had failed to indict Clive, the Secret Committee had succeeded in giving the Government some control over the affairs of the East India Company. By the Regulating Act of 1773 the Government forced upon the Company, in exchange for a £1,000,000 loan, much needed reforms. Ironically, many of them had already been suggested by Clive; though the most important one, power of the Governor-General to overrule his Council, was withheld. A fact that was to cause, in time, many troubles to Clive's successor, Warren Hastings.

So the year-long struggle against Sullivan was over. Clive was secure in his fortune, happy in his marriage, his honour intact. He was in the prime of life.

Lord North, indolent but devious, was thinking once again of making him Commander-in-Chief of the British forces that would shortly be needed in America. The famous 'Boston tea party' had just taken place there. Who could tell what this General, who had never lost even a single battle, could do in that vast but sparsely populated land, seething now with rebellion? Could not the far-seeing administrator that he was bring peace where no one else could do so?

These were questions never to be answered. Clive's health had not improved since his return to England. He had, through sheer will power, held his illness at bay during the long struggle in Parliament.

But now that he had won, it returned with added violence. His gallstones gave him no rest. There was hardly a moment when he was not in pain. Despite visits to spas, despite the increasing use of opium, there was nothing he could do to alleviate the pain.

With the danger of defeat removed, he became increasingly depressed. As in his youth, inactivity brought on the moods of utter despair.

He struggled on for another year, taking more and more drugs, depending almost entirely for relief on massive doses of morphia and laudanum.

About the middle of November 1774, he wrote to a friend: 'How miserable is my condition. I have a disease which makes life insupportable, but which doctors tell me won't shorten it an hour.'

And yet, a few days later, on 22 November 1774, he was dead. He was a little more than forty-nine.

Although the newspapers of the day announced that he 'died of an overdose of opium unwittingly taken', immediately the most extravagant rumours began to circulate. For, even now, it was as if this remarkable man with his extraordinary life could not be allowed to die a natural death.

It must be something, like the whole of his life, dramatic and unusual. What else could it be but suicide?

The favourite story of the day went something like this.

A woman friend of his wife's was staying with them in their Berkeley Square house. He had suffered more severely than usual from the pain of the gallstones, taken greater doses of laudanum than ever.

At about noon on the twenty-second, this guest came into Clive's room, holding out one of the feather plumes used for writing.

She complained that she could not find a decent pen, and that the one she held was blunt.

'Would you be so good', she asked, 'as to mend this one?'

'Certainly', he replied, and taking the feather from her, went across the window. He took a penknife out of his pocket and sharpened the quill for her.

She thanked him, and then left.

Shortly afterwards he was found by one of his servants with his throat cut, with the same small knife.

Another version of the same tale insisted that he was playing whist, and that at a certain point in the game, he got up and left the room.

When he did not return, Margaret went out to look for him, and found him in another room with his throat cut.

It seemed that everyone was determined that he should die by his own hand, that this was the only possible death for one who had attempted it before, and defied death so long in so many places.

The suicide theory gained ground because of the silence maintained by his family and by the secrecy of his burial at Moreton Say.

But though fashionable London would have no other solution but a dramatic suicide, a much less unusual but more plausible account was also circulating.

It was that Clive was waiting in that dressing-room of his in Berkeley Square for a coach to take him to yet another visit to Bath, when he suddenly had one of his usual spasms of pain.

He immediately took a large dose of laudanum. Like many people who are in the habit of taking drugs, he did not realise that he had reached the stage where even a moderate dose could be fatal.

He did not die from a self-inflicted wound. He did not cut his throat.

He died of a heart attack brought on by an overdose of drugs.

The family remained silent to hide not his suicide, but the fact that he had become a drug-addict.

Even in Moreton Say, the stories flew. It was said that he had shot himself under a magnolia tree; and that, as suicides should be, he was buried at the intersection of a cross-roads.

Credence to these tales was added by the fact that nobody knew, for years, where he was buried. He was certainly not in the square family mausoleum in the churchyard. With his widow remaining silent mainly at Oakly Park, for the forty-three years she was to outlive her husband; with the family taking on the title of Powis, with the name of Clive being slowly eradicated, the mystery remained.

It was not until the end of the nineteenth century that further information came to light. Lady Margaret Herbert was fond of the small Saxon church at Moreton Say that had been refaced with brick, known as Flemish bonding, late in the eighteenth century. But she felt that it should be renovated again, and gave instructions that various works were to be carried out.

One of the tasks was to replace the old stone slabs inside the church with a more elegant parquet flooring.

When the workmen prised up the slabs in front of the chancel, they found Clive's lead coffin. And when they put down the parquet flooring they left it there, at the spot where, today, the lectern stands.

Lady Margaret Herbert had a small, not very flamboyant, brass tablet put up on the church wall. It had the following inscription:

> *Sacred to the memory*
> *of*
> *Robert Lord Clive KB*
> *buried within the walls*
> *of this church*
> *Born Sep 29 1725*
> *Died Nov 22 1774*
> *Primus in Indis*

It is argued that a suicide, however important, could not have been buried inside a church itself.

Besides, he had no cause for conscious suicide. He had defeated his enemies. His fortune was safe. He was busy with his new houses. He was happy with his wife. She had stood by him in India and in England, supporting him, nursing him, encouraging him. Not once had she let him down.

When he died, his eldest son Edward, who was one day to become the Earl of Powis, was twenty. His daughter Rebecca was fourteen. Another daughter, Charlotte, twelve, a third, Margaret, eleven, and his youngest son, Robert, five.

218

Married men, with families of young children to bring up, rarely commit suicide. But any man or woman, in long and desperate pain, accustomed to taking pain-relieving drugs, can give themselves that one ounce too much that is fatal.

But in death, as in life, everything about Robert Clive had to be different. So a fictitious end was given to his life in order to comply with the exceptional facts of his life. It seemed the only thing to do.

INDEX